Seeing Yourself Through God's Eyes

beautiful

D1607236

Angela Thomas

TRANSIT®

www.TransitBooks.com
A Division of Thomas Nelson, Inc.
www.ThomasNelson.com

Published in Nashville, Tennessee, by Tommy Nelson®, a Division of Thomas Nelson, Inc.

Adapted from *Do You Think I'm Beautiful?* and *Do You Think I'm Beautiful Bible Study &
Journal* by Angela Thomas

Unless otherwise noted, Scripture quotations are from the HOLY BIBLE: NEW INTERNA-
TIONAL VERSION®. Copyright © 1973, 1978, 1984 by International Bible Society. Used by
permission of Zondervan Publishing House. All rights reserved.

Scripture quotations noted NKJV are from THE NEW KING JAMES VERSION. Copyright ©
1979, 1980, 1982, Thomas Nelson Publishers, Inc.

Scripture quotations noted The Message are from *The Message* by Eugene H. Peterson,
copyright © 1993, 1994, 1995, 1996, 2000, 2001, 2002. Used by permission of NavPress
Publishing Group. All rights reserved.

Library of Congress Cataloging-in-Publication Data

Thomas, Angela, 1962-
   Beautiful / Angela Thomas.
      p. cm.
   Includes bibliographical references.
      ISBN 1-4003-0426-1 (softcover with cd)
      1. Teenage girls—Religious life—Juvenile literature. 2. Christian
life—Juvenile literature. I. Title.
BV4551.3.T48 2004
248.8'33—dc22

                                                                    2004011932

Printed in the United States of America

04 05 06 07 08 WOR 9 8 7 6 5 4 3 2

For Taylor and AnnaGrace . . .

You are beautiful.

Contents

If there is a question attached to a girl's soul, maybe it's **"Do You Think I'm Beautiful?"** 1 When God answers from the depth of His great love, it makes some of us feel like **The Wallflower Who Is Asked to Dance** 13. But we can become distracted from His invitation because of **The Other Loves** 29, **Whispers of Unbelief** 43, **Noise and Clutter** 57, and because we are **Sometimes the Prodigal, Sometimes the Elder Brother** 71.

To return to the music and strong embrace of God requires **A Desperate and Pursuing Heart** 93. And when a girl chooses to remain in His arms of devotion, God gives **The Only Hope We Have** 111, **His Perfect Love** 129, and **A Beautiful Crown** 147.

God is enthralled by the beauty of a woman and calls her His beloved. He wildly pursues her heart with romance and intimacy to make her **His Beautiful Bride** 165.

If there is a question attached to a girl's soul,

maybe it's "Do you think I'm beautiful?"

Chapter 1

Do You Think I'm Beautiful?

I've worn glasses since I was eighteen months old. My first pair had cat-eye frames, and everyone thought I looked so cute in them. "Oh, look at that little baby with glasses. Isn't she the sweetest thing?" Then I began to grow, and for about a year, I had to wear a patch over my right eye to make the left one stronger. I guess it was a decent idea, but it didn't work. It caused my weaker eye to become the dominant one. Don't you know I was a stunner in the Captain Hook patch with cat-eye glasses on top?

In elementary school, kids tagged me, of course, "four eyes." I was special—one of maybe three "four eyes" in the entire school. Me and my wire-rim, stop-sign-shaped glasses. How cool can a girl be with traffic signs in front of her eyes? Not very. And a few years later, for the full effect, my frames got bigger, and we added three and a half years of braces. *Railroad tracks. Tinsel teeth.* That was me . . . thick bottle caps before my eyes, tin on my teeth, and—to make things as awful as possible—I was smart. Girls don't want to be smart in junior high. They just want to be pretty.

By the time junior high rolled around, I knew for sure that beauty had eluded me. Now, my best friend, Carla, she was beautiful. Some senior guy even asked her to the prom when we were in the *eighth* grade. The eighth grade! Can you imagine that? Carla was at the high school prom, and I was at home writing a paper. Yep, there were many beautiful girls at my school, but I was not among them. I could do algebra and remember the answers for history tests. I actually did all of my homework and turned it in on time. I would make up practice tests, take the tests, and then grade them—all to prepare for the actual thing. What a dweeb!

All I really wanted was to look like everyone else, but my circumstances wouldn't cooperate. Long, thick, straight hair that I styled with two barrettes every day of my young life. Braces that seemed destined to be a permanent part of my smile. And the doom of "four eyes" forever. Don't get the wrong impression; no one ever called me ugly, and no one ever laughed in my face. It's just that no one ever noticed.

The Plain One

I have fumbled along with this beauty thing ever since those elementary days. I eventually realized that if I couldn't appeal to their visual senses, I could make people laugh and be fun enough to appeal to their hearts. I became a cheerleader and an all-around great friend. *Steady.* That's what most people called me. You could count on me to show up on time, make good decisions, and always, always, always try to do the right thing. I was the one who would stand with you no matter what, the one you could snub one day and hug the next without so much as an apology. There were no boyfriends to distract me from my friends or academics, and, besides, who *doesn't* need a friend as faithful as a golden retriever? As long as they'd pat me on the head every once in a while, I'd run and fetch and do just about anything to please.

Every Sunday on the way to church, my daddy would say he had the prettiest daughter in the whole wide world. I know: it was sweet. But that's what dad's are supposed to say, right? I heard him and have held on to his words to this day, but deep down, back then, I didn't believe him. If I were really pretty, I reasoned, then someone besides my father would notice. But no one ever did.

When compliments were handed out, I was an afterthought. "Wow, Carla, you look amazing in that outfit! . . . Angela, you look nice too." I felt like saying, "Please, don't bother. You're only highlighting the obvious." I remember the high school quarterback calling my name, saying he wanted to talk to me, and then asking if I thought my friend would go out with him. Sound familiar? Happened more times than I can count. It makes me smile now, but I can also still feel the emptiness in my stomach as I reminisce.

List ten adjectives that describe you from the inside out.

1. _____
2. _____
3. _____
4. _____
5. _____
6. _____
7. _____
8. _____
9. _____
10. _____

Did you include the word *beautiful* in your description?
Why or why not?

_____
_____
_____

3

It was simply a predetermined fact that I could not control: I was not beautiful. Unless you asked my grandmother, who'd tell you, "Pretty is as pretty does." Of course, that's Southern for, "Well, you are kind of homely, but try not to think about it." God bless my grandmother for always keeping my feet firmly anchored in the ground.

I realize that I have painted a fairly depressing picture here. Homely, brainy nerd compensates by going out for the cheerleading squad, Velcro-ing herself to some friends, and trying always to do the right thing—but still gets lost in the crowd. Depressing, but accurate. Almost.

You see, the summer before my senior year in high school, I discovered contact lenses, got my braces off, and tried a cool, new haircut—all within a week or so. My best friend sat beside me at a baseball game and literally didn't recognize me. I'd wave to friends at the mall, and they wouldn't wave back. Completely changed on the outside. Maybe even pretty if you tilted your head and squinted. But the die had already been cast on the inside. I knew that I would never be beautiful.

Groovin' from the Edge

I know you know the story of Cinderella. The evil stepsisters and their mother are at the ball along with all the other available bachelorettes in the kingdom. Prince Charming is becoming discouraged because he has met every bride wanna-be, but no one has captured his heart. Thankfully, there is a fairy godmother, and after a little bibbity-bobbity-boo, Cinderella finally arrives. She is breathtaking, and the entire room is captivated by her beauty. Prince Charming is eternally smitten. There is a night of dancing, a quick goodbye, a shoe that fits, and a happily ever after.

Now tell me, when you think of yourself in this story,

which character do you allow yourself to become? Where are you standing at the ball? I would love it if you thought of yourself as Cinderella. I have tried on those slippers but have never been able to bring myself to believe that I should be dancing in her shoes. I have never thought of myself as a stepsister or the evil stepmother either. Somehow, I have always seen myself as one of the faceless in the crowd. One of the girls from the kingdom who gave it her best shot, spent days preparing for the ball, splurged on the dress and the hair, and anxiously arrived with butterflies in her stomach, only to stand around with the other hopefuls, make small talk, smile politely, groove to the music, and remain unnoticed.

I have a friend who said to me, "Angela, I think that's a bunch of bull. I can't believe you could really feel like that." Actually, it would be bull to tell you differently. Oh, I *want* to be Cinderella. I want to be the most beautiful woman at the ball, but I've never been bold enough to think of myself as her. Maybe it's those memories of junior high. Maybe I've been conditioned by my environment. Maybe I'm just a coward. Whichever it is, when you grow up longing to be beautiful but knowing that you are not, it feels like there could never be a glass slipper that would fit.

Most of us took different paths but arrived at the same conclusion: Cinderella is always someone else. There is a little girl inside me who secretly aches for a fairy godmother to magically bumble her way into my life, wave her wand, and make me into the

Which character do you allow yourself to become?

princess I have always longed to be. Make me beautiful. Make me captivating. Make someone notice.

But life is not a fairy tale. Magic wands are only for pretending. Cinderella shoes are mass-produced by the millions for the tiny feet of little girls who still believe Prince Charming will ask them to dance. But sensible girls wear sensible shoes, put their ball gowns in storage, and teach themselves to believe that being asked to dance isn't all that important anyway.

I have spent way too much time standing around the edge of my life trying to convince myself that I do not want to be Cinderella, pretending that I really didn't come to dance. I have concocted a few lies to make life hurt less and then forced myself to live them. Besides, glass slippers probably pinch your toes.

> The God who slung the stars across the heavens . . . the same One who shaped the mountains and valleys with the palm of His hand . . . the God whose very breath gives life . . . that God, the King, has always been taken with you. You have been noticed, He thinks you're beautiful, the glass slipper fits, the music is playing, and He's asking you to dance.

When No One Notices

I don't think this is just my story. I truly believe that the longing to be known as beautiful is a part of our design as girls. God put us together this way on purpose. We are wired to long for beauty, yet the world does a wonderful job of squelching this desire. I realized over time that I could not have anything in life that required me to be beautiful. I understood almost instinctively that I should keep my head down, study hard, try to do the right thing, and maybe life would turn out okay in the end.

The journey, of course, can play out in many ways. Your experience may be quite different from mine. My friends who have been beautiful on the outside all of their lives have struggles that are foreign to me. Because they have been noticed for their physical beauty, they fear that no one will ever see their heart or their true self. Or they fear that they will be accepted only because of their beauty and will be rejected if anyone ever looks below the surface. I have a beautiful friend who has anxiety attacks in church because she is afraid that everyone is looking at her. Although it is painfully real for her, it is no exaggeration to say I cannot imagine her struggle. You see, I have always assumed that no one is looking.

And so, when no one notices, a lot of us wander through life blending in, always trying to figure out the balance of being just right, like boiled eggs—bland and easy to swallow. Other girls act out, doing anything to get someone to notice. But either way, after lost hope, the ache of disappointment, and the repetitive pain of rejection, the longing to be beautiful is buried and the insecurities grow. The desire to be known as beautiful is eventually stuffed away into an untouchable place in our hearts.

We cannot deny that the desire is there—whether you are like my friends or like me. It has been there for every girl I've ever known. Deep down, we long for romance. We long to be rescued. We long for a hero to steal us away. We long to be beautiful.

Do you hear me saying that I long to be weak and brainless? Then you have not heard me. I want to be incredibly intelligent, creative, and significant. It's just that when I let myself search for the truth of my

> Do you hear me saying that I long to be weak and brainless?

7

heart, it's always in the voice of a little girl who wants to grow up and be beautiful one day too. It feels a little goofy to be wrestling with these truths. But better now than never at all.

Maybe no one has ever really noticed you either. And you've learned to pretend that it's okay. *It's not okay!* You were made to be seen and known and loved deeply. And it's okay to want what you were made for.

No More Pretending

We all pretend for a while or for a lifetime. But pretending is not living. It's like wearing a designer snow parka and sitting in the lodge but never really skiing down the mountain. When we pretend, we are alive and present, maybe sipping hot chocolate by the fire, but missing the whole extent of what God intended for our lives.

Have you ever heard your heart cry, "Do you think I'm beautiful?" Then let these words embrace you with their truth:

The king is enthralled by your beauty. Psalm 45:11

Eventually, there was a day when it was just me and God with my insecurity. Everything had hit me at once, and I was crying; actually, I was sobbing like a baby. My heart was racing, and my chest felt like it was going to explode. And finally, through a blur of tears, these words made their way into my journal:

Oh, God, do You think I'm beautiful?

No one else has been able . . . so is it You? There is so much more inside of me, a great well of passion and dreams. A place I never let myself go. Is it safe to trust You with the rest of my heart? What will You do with me if I show You everything? Every desire? Every longing? Every doubt? Every weakness? If I show You, will You still love me? Will You hold me and care for me in the dark?

Oh, God, hold me, please hold me and tell me that You love me. Tell me that You'll fight for me. Tell me that I am beautiful.

I cried and waited. Empty. I lay on the floor completely spent. The question took up the whole room, and there was nothing else to say, except to pray:

It's just me.

You see it all. You know it's just me. You know how You've made me, and You know how to speak so that I can hear.

I cannot move until I hear from You.

In the wilderness of that room, as alone as I have ever been, the Lord met me. The words He formed in my mind began to answer the question. In my imagination, I could sense the Lord patiently smiling over me, and I heard Him speak into my heart:

Yes, Angela, I think that you are beautiful. Your desire has served its purpose; you have finally brought your true heart to Me. Are you tired of pretending? Are you tired of hoping that someone else could fill the place that was meant for Me? I see you, all of you, and you do not have to hide anymore. I see your sin and I see your flaws and I still desire you as My own. I am crazy about you. I am the answer. The "more" that your heart waits for is Me.

Yes, dear one, yes, you are incredibly beautiful to Me.

Now it's your turn. (Dog-ear this page because you're going to be coming back!) Ask God if He thinks you're beautiful, then boldly request an answer. Ask God to be loud when He answers. Ask Him to speak to you in ways that are unmistakable! When He answers—and He will—come back here and record what He says.

My Prayer   Date:

_____

_____

_____

God's Answer   Date:

_____

_____

_____

While you await His answer, take some time to look up these passages in the Bible. What is God trying to tell you through these Scriptures?

John 8:32

_____

_____

Psalm 51:6

_____

_____

Philippians 4:8

_____

_____

If there is a question attached to a girl's soul,

maybe it's "Do you think I'm beautiful?"

When God answers from the depth of

His great love, it makes some of us feel like

the wallflower who is asked to dance.

Chapter 2

The Wallflower Who Is Asked to Dance

Kerry Gibson was the newest, cutest guy on the scene when I was in the eleventh grade. He went to a high school across town, and a lot of the girls at my school had fallen for his million-dollar smile and that every-mother-would-love-him charm. I had seen Kerry Gibson entertaining the girls after football games at Sir Pizza, but Kerry Gibson had never seen me. As a matter of fact, he had no idea that I existed.

I think it was sometime around February that year when a new teen dance club opened. One Saturday, my committee of girlfriends spent the whole day deciding what each of us should wear, calling to see who else was planning to go, and worrying about our hair until there was no use and we just had to go with the hair we had. I was looking forward to being with my friends, laughing, sipping a soda, and as usual, watching everyone else dance the night away.

At some point that night, my circle of friends huddled

together, talking to a few of the guys from our school. Over walked Handsome in a pair of Levi's. You guessed it—Kerry Gibson. He grinned and said to the guy standing next to me, "Mind if I dance with your date?"

The guy beside me couldn't get it out fast enough: "Man, she's not with me." And our whole circle stood there with mouths agape as if to say, "Kerry, are you sure? It sounds like you're asking Angela to dance." I was the most dumbfounded of all. It felt like a dream I'd had a million times: the cutest guy in the room was asking me to dance. I stood there, patiently waiting to wake up. There was no way that Kerry Gibson had just asked *me* to dance.

"Hey, I'm Kerry." Reality was intersecting with a dream. "Do you want to dance?"

"Okay," I mumbled, realizing that every person who knew me was staring in disbelief. The wallflower had just been asked to dance. I don't remember breathing. I was so afraid of ruining the whole thing.

Well, we danced. I wish I could remember the song. Some late-seventies disco number. And I'm telling you, I could dance. I had practiced in my room for years, and not one cool move had been wasted. But the song was over way too soon. His act of charity was coming to an end. I could feel it—the good deed was over. I smiled at Kerry, said, "Thanks for the dance," and turned to walk away. But then, bless him—I mean it, God bless him—Kerry Gibson said, "Wait, do you want to keep dancing?" I think I nodded yes, and we danced every dance until I had to go home.

Do you want to keep dancing? The question still rings in my head. It makes me cry and smile and whisper a prayer for girls everywhere: "God, make sure someone asks them to keep dancing."

When was the first time you were asked to dance? You know the crazy thing that happens in your stomach when a cute guy walks toward you? What *is* that? And why does it make us feel like we're floating? Are you smiling? I am.

A good part of my life has been like that night. I know that I am at the dance. I see everyone else having a great time. I am enjoying the music and the people. But I'm not really sure anyone sees me. I am polite and fun . . . and hesitant. Maybe I'm always supposed to stand in the back and wave to my friends at the front. Maybe my life is supposed to be a supporting role. I have wondered if I was made to be a wallflower. And I have told myself that it would be okay if I were.

I've never been sure that someone would walk across that dance floor and call my name. There have been seasons when I decided my life was supposed to be that way. Everyone else got pulled onto the dance floor, and some were even bold enough to run out and boogie by themselves, but I couldn't. Maybe it just wasn't meant for me. I felt my feet want to. It sure did look like fun. "Nah," I'd tell myself. "Quit dreaming about dancing and go do your homework."

When God Walks Across the Room

Here's what I've learned about God: there are no faceless girls standing around the edge of the room with Him. He did not bring you to the dance just to shove you into a corner and tell you to have a great time watching. You were made for strobe lights, and you do not have to shuffle around in the shadows hoping that one day it'll be your turn.

You are not just one of the crowd. God sees you, and He sees me. He walks across the room, looks directly at

Maybe the thoughts of romance have been ruined for you. An awful relationship, terrible memories of molestation, or worse. Did you know that God never intended for romance to be ugly? He meant for this kind of intimacy to be pure and painless. If you need to, would you ask Him, right here, to begin changing the ideas you associate with romance.

_____

_____

_____

_____

_____

_____

_____

_____

_____

_____

Angela,

I am really struggling with remembering my story. From my earliest memories, I have been called beautiful. I remember at the age of four being told that I was pretty just before I was molested. I never wanted to be beautiful anymore.

—Erin

you, and says that you are beautiful. You are not a wanna-be to Him, and neither am I. He calls out every wallflower, I mean every single one, and asks her to dance.

Do you know what the dance is? The dance is your life. The dance is you in the arms of God, gliding around the center of the room, becoming the woman He thought of when He dreamed of you. To dance is to say, "I can do that," and then to magnificently step out into the strength of God's call and shine. To dance is to grab hold of what you were made to be and then let Him show you how to *become*.

Into Your Eyes

When God looks into your eyes, He sees all the beauty that He created there. He sees every potential and every gift. He sees what can be and redeems what has been. He loves the curly hair that you wish were straight. He is taken with your smile and the shape of your nose. He's crazy about big feet and knobby knees and every curve that is particular to you. He is the One who loves the inside *and* the outside of you. You were all His idea, and you are physically and emotionally beautiful to Him.

Do you want to dance? Does your heart cry out, "Does anyone see me? Do you think I'm beautiful?" Then hear again Psalm 45:11: The king is *enthralled by your beauty*. (Emphasis mine.)

Enthralled by your beauty. That

> Quick! Without reading the words, just write your name in the blank. Now go back and read the message God has for YOU!
>
> Listen, _____, consider
> and give ear:
> Forget your people and your
> father's house.
> The king is enthralled with your
> beauty;
> Honor him, for he is your Lord.
>
> Psalm 45:10–11

God has seen you across the room, and He cannot take His eyes off you.

means captivated, smitten, fascinated, spellbound, and delighted. That's exactly how the prince feels about the princess in fairy tales. But this sentiment is not fiction. Enthralled is how God in heaven feels about you. He is taken with you. Undistracted. Intensely interested. Emotionally connected. He enjoys your laughter and takes pleasure in the way you think. He is not bored with you, and He would never consider you ordinary. There is no way you will ever go unnoticed with God. You are beautiful to Him. Incredibly, breathtakingly beautiful. When a man feels this way about a woman, we say he's "in love."

You have heard that God loves you, but maybe you have been like me and misunderstood. His love for you is not just a "whole world in His hands" kind of love. This love is individual. God and you. One-on-one. Personal. God's love for you is pure and without reservation. He never holds back or plays games with your heart. There are no riddles with God. This kind of love does not stand you up. He always shows up, always remembers, and always keeps His promises. God's love is unrelenting. He does not turn away even if you do. His excitement over you does not wane. God's love is not some kindergarten crush. He is not fickle. God has seen you across the room, and He cannot take His eyes off you.

Do you get this? Do you hear me describing the love that you long for on this earth? Does this sound like the love you have been looking for? Maybe you have tasted this love in relationships, yet you recognize that there is still a deeper longing. Is your heart pounding, "Yes, that's the love I have imagined"? Our desires reflect our design. The love that God has for us is the love your soul was made for. It is an intimate, vulnerable, completing kind of love.

Have you ever considered that
enthralled is how God feels about you? Do
you hesitate when you hear these ideas? What holds
you back?

_____

_____

_____

_____

_____

The God Thing

A few months ago, I spent three hours in a chair at my salon while a guy painted strands of my hair with five different colors of blonde. I was there a long time, and the regular conversation about family, holidays, and the weather had been spent. He asked what I was working on. Forgetting that I was robed in black with alien hair, I said, "It's a book called *Do You Think I'm Beautiful?*" (I was working on the women's book at the time.)

We both looked into the mirror and laughed.

"What's it about?" he asked.

"Well, it's about having permission to ask the question of beauty and then coming to understand what life can be like when a woman finally believes that God is wild about her. Knowing that He thinks she is beautiful gives strength and confidence and peace."

"Angela, why can't it just be about self-esteem and hanging in there? You know, picking-yourself-up-and-dusting-yourself-off kind of stuff. Get your act together and get with it. Why does it have to be about the God thing?"

I smiled, took a big swig of my Sprite, and jumped in.

Maybe you feel like that too. *Why does it have to be about the God thing?* It has to be about the God thing because all the other things haven't worked. Hands down. No questions. I meet women all the time—hey, I *am* one of those women—who have tried everything else and at the end of the day ask, "Is that it? That's all there is?"

The only Person who has ever brought sustained power and purpose into my life is the living person of God. The only words that keep making sense are His words. The only way that always stands is His way. Many years ago, I had to decide what I was going to do with the God thing. I made a conscious decision to believe. Every day, I keep deciding to believe. Sometimes I believe because I actually see God working out His plan. Sometimes it's because I have studied and believe even more. And then some days, I choose to keep believing by faith—faith that He is actually there and real and moving even when I can't see Him.

Maybe this God thing is new to you, and you don't know very much about the One who has asked you to dance. Maybe this all sounds kind of hokey. Maybe you don't know this God who thinks you are beautiful and loves you personally. Or maybe you have been introduced but remain distant. I would ask you, has anything ever come close to filling the depths of your heart? Have you ever known a love or beauty that sustained you? Can

> It has to be about the God thing because all the other things haven't worked.

you make sense of it all by yourself? Then maybe what's missing, in fact, is God.

To believe in God is the beginning. To hear Him call your name is the start. To dance in His arms is real life. The music will be fast, then slow, then fast. The steps will be both easy and complex. The lights will be sometimes bright and sometimes dim. But to miss Him and to miss the dance is to miss the life you were made for.

To finally connect with God—to believe that God is really who He said He is—will make you feel like the wallflower who is asked to dance.

Following His Lead

When I got to college, there were a few rites of passage my freshman year in an all-girls dorm. Camping out overnight for basketball tickets. Panty raids. Syllabi shock. And learning to shag dance. My friend Lisa had an older sister who taught her how, and we spent most of our study breaks out in the hall singing and practicing our smooth moves.

There was a guy named Jack who asked me out that year. I don't know where he learned, but that boy could dance. I loved dancing with him because he made it fun. He was totally in charge and confident. Smiling all the time and singing at the top of his lungs. I'd come off the dance floor, and my friends would say, "Wow, you guys are really good together." The reason we were so good together had very little to do with me. Jack was great, and I would just follow his lead.

I was green as a gourd when it came to shag dancing, but Jack was so stinking sure of himself. He would turn me where he wanted me to turn. He'd give me this little look, as if to say, "Here we go," and I'd just hang on. Every song was another lesson, and I kept learning. When I'd step on his toes, he would just laugh and give that same spin another try. Dancing with him made me feel beautiful, and all I had to do was follow.

When God says, "Come dance with Me," He is not saying you have to know all the steps. This is the God of all creation who provides the music, sets the stage, takes you by the hand, and then leads. If you will rest in His arms, you can trust every turn that He takes. You do not have to be embarrassed to learn because He is a patient teacher. You do not have to look behind you to see where you are going because you can trust that He is watching.

As a little girl, I would stand on my daddy's feet and dance with him. God lets us do that too. You can put your feet on His, and He will carry you around the room. Eventually, His steps will become yours, and you can allow yourself to be swept away by the music. You are beautiful in His arms. Dancing is fun. Your job is easy: rest in His strong embrace and follow His lead.

The Other Questions

Since beginning to dance with God and getting the hang of following, I have been learning more and more of His love for you and me. In His arms, I've found permission to ask all the questions that have rattled around in my heart. "Do You think I'm beautiful?" seemed to capture the essence of my longings, but more questions have since spilled out. Are they meant to be answered by God too? I believe that they are.

His words are found in the Bible, and, believing they are true, I have gone there to find His answers for my questions.

> **Q:** Does anyone notice me?!
>
> **A:** The eyes of the Lord are on the righteous and his ears are attentive to their cry. Psalm 34:15
>
> **Q:** Is anyone listening to me???
>
> **A:** The Lord is near to all who call upon Him. Psalm 145:18 NKJV
>
> **Q:** Will You rescue me?
>
> **A:** He rescued me from my powerful enemy, from my foes, who were too strong for me. They confronted me in the day of my disaster, but the Lord was my support. He brought me out into a spacious place; *he rescued me because he delighted in me.* Psalm 18:17–19 (emphasis mine)

And the Biggie: *Do You Really Love Me?*

I guess this is the question that prompts every longing in our hearts: "Do you really love me?" Girls grow up wondering, *Do you really love me? Daddy, do you see me dancing in my party dress and smile with delight over me?* When dads are distant or abusive or addicted or just not affectionate, girls grow to be insecure and decide to ask their question of other guys—except this time the question becomes, "Will you love me *if* . . . ?" Will you love me if I sleep with you? Will you love me if I do drugs with you? Will you love me if I lie for you? Will you love me if I prop you up?

Those girls discover a few answers that seem to add something to the empty cup of their souls, like a few drops of water into a dusty tin can. The cup never gets filled, but there is a momentary satisfaction that mimics thirst being quenched.

I cannot avoid the deep longing in my own heart. Do you really love me? means, Will you accept me? Will you embrace what is different about me and applaud my efforts? Can I just be human? Can I be myself? Can I be honest and expect honesty? Is it okay if I have a bad haircut, a protruding zit, or last year's trends? Will you love me even if I disappoint you? Will you love me through dark places? Will you love me even when I doubt your love?

Sometimes we taste this love in our lifetime. Our parents can love us with a pure love. A boyfriend can give a profound love. A friend can spend a lifetime embracing us with unshakable love. But here is the catch about the design of our souls: the love we know here on earth will never be enough. We have been made by God *for* God. To operate with only the taste of love we get on earth will leave us incomplete. That's by design. Our hearts have been made to cry out for a love that can come only from our Creator. The cup of our soul will never be filled apart from the love of God.

God's love is love that never fails. The unfailing love that we desire comes from Him. His love runs toward me, even when I am unlovely. His love comes to find me when I am hiding. His love will not let me go. His love never ends. His love never fails.

Are there empty places in your heart that no person or thing has ever been able to fill? There are holes in our heart and soul. We can see them

> Love is patient, love is kind. It does not envy, it does not boast, it is not proud. It is not rude, it is not self-seeking, it is not easily angered, it keeps no record of wrongs. Love does not delight in evil but rejoices with the truth. It always protects, always trusts, always hopes, always perseveres. Love never fails.
>
> 1 Corinthians
> 13:4–8

now. Deep, dark, desolate holes. The love we have tasted has not filled these places. Filling those holes requires the lavish, unfailing love of God.

The Lord hears you cry from those empty places, "Do You really love me?" And over and over throughout Scripture, He tenderly speaks to us:

If you could only grasp how wide and how long and how high and how deep, then you'd know, yes, I really love you.

Do you wonder if you are too far away from Me? My love is wider still.

Do you think that you've been away too long? My love will wait longer.

Do you believe that no one would ever want someone like you? My love is higher than all the others.

Have you been sure that you are too far gone? My love is deep enough to reach even you.

You cannot fall past My love.

You cannot outrun My love.

You cannot reach the end of My love. It is wide and long and high and deep enough for you.

Go Ahead and Dance

I know you may want to hesitate. I sure have. Too many times. But you have to believe me here. The God of

> What are you learning about the God thing? Why is He the only way we will ever find answers to our questions?
>
> _____
>
> _____
>
> _____
>
> _____

heaven sees you. He wants you as His own. His is the relationship you long for. You just have to say yes. Push past your fear. Forget about those two left feet. Don't worry about who's watching. Go ahead and dance with Him.

When you are dancing with God, you are held in the arms of unfailing love. There is intimacy there . . . the freedom to whisper truths . . . ask unspoken questions . . . the acceptance to speak about the longings of your soul . . . a give-and-take relationship that leads to deeper understanding and deeper love and deeper strength.

When a wallflower is asked to dance, it feels like the earth moves and time stands still while a dream unfolds. That empty, alone feeling evaporates. In that moment, the wallflower feels like someone is finally saying to her, "I see you over there. I think that you are beautiful. Come with me into the center of the room. Don't run away. Let's keep dancing."

That is what God is doing. He is calling your name. He has chosen your favorite music. He looks at you with devotion and affection. He takes you into His strong arms and leads you around the floor. This is romance, pure and simple. This is enduring, unfailing love . . . the completing love your heart longs for.

Have you heard God call your name? Have you felt

that He is saying, "I have more for you"? Then what are you afraid of? Sometimes we're afraid to dance when we don't know the steps. Remember that you don't have to know the tango or the rumba. It will be fun to follow His lead. Stand on His feet. Feel the music. Watch as He turns you and learn.

Would you rest in the embrace of your Lord? This moment with Him will not fade. It's time to begin dancing the dance of your life. He thinks that you are extraordinarily beautiful. Did you hear that? You. Now whip out those groovy moves and enjoy His great delight.

If there is a question attached to a girl's soul, maybe it's "Do you think I'm beautiful?" When God answers from the depth of His great love, it makes some of us feel like the wallflower who is asked to dance.

But we can become distracted from His invitation because of the other loves.

Chapter 3

The Other Loves

The night Kerry Gibson asked me to dance was so powerful that I can still remember almost every detail many years later. As a matter of fact, if I stopped and thought about it, I could probably recall the particulars of meeting each of the boyfriends I've had. What they said. What I said. Where we were. I might even be able to tell you what I was wearing.

Not long after my senior year began, Kerry showed up at a football game where I was cheering. All of the girls whispered down the line, "Guess who's here? Up in the bleachers near the band . . . it looks like Kerry Gibson. What is he doing at our school?" He said hello to me later and then called the next day. I think I expected him to ask for someone else's number, but surprisingly he asked me out. That weekend there was a first date, then lazy afternoons of nervous giggles on the phone, and before long, we were "going together." I remember feeling as if I were floating for a whole year. Kerry was my first boyfriend, and I was smitten. I'd see him across the room, and my heart would skip. I'd hear him call my name and almost lose my breath. Puppy love, I guess. But wow, all those goofy feelings were fun.

I can't remember a thing I learned in French class, but I can still remember the boys' names I wrote on my note-books. What is the deal with me? Why are all the silly whims of my heart stuck inside my head? Does this happen to anyone else? Am I the goofiest person in the world? I may be going out on a limb here, but I guess that if the truth were told, you could remember too. Maybe not word for word, or moment by moment, but most likely, emotionally you could remember well. It seems like girls have been designed to give special attention to matters of the heart and then hold them close, even for a lifetime.

Do you remember the first time you were kissed? Not like that silly kiss I got in the second grade when a guy on the bus paid Tommy Sands a quarter to kiss me and run. That one just about ruined my entire life. The whole bus laughed. I cried and ran home. Tommy got twenty-five cents, and I was too embarrassed to ever show my face on the bus again.

Nope, that's not the kiss I'm talking about. I'm talking about the KA-BOOM kiss, the one that made your knees go weak. The kiss where you closed your eyes and thought for sure that you were in heaven. It was the moment when you finally knew what it felt like to be desired by someone you desired. It was the kiss that you didn't want to end. And that kiss is the one you've been chasing ever since. You can't tell me any different; I won't believe it if you try.

What is that inside a woman? We want feelings that we can't govern. The ones that come into our hearts and take hold of everything. The feelings that make us too sick to eat and too consumed to make good sense. We want to be as giddy as Miss Scarlett with Rhett Butler. We want passion to go on forever, and we'll resign ourselves to read about it or watch it in a movie if we can't really have it. The intense longing for romance and relationship. An incredible craving to be seen and known and desired. Whether we admit it or not, each of us came wired so very much alike—feminine, relational, feeling, and yearning for the arms of a true love.

The Other Loves

If I am supposed to be dancing in the arms of God and He is supposed to be enough, then why this intense need for others to love me? What is the role of the other people who love me, the other loves in my heart and life? Why do girls spend their lives pining for the affections of guys? Why do we hold on to the memories of what we have experienced and the fantasies of what could be? Why does it even matter if they notice or if they call us beautiful? Why did we believe that a guy would be the answer, and if the first one wasn't then maybe the second one or even the third one will be?

Remember our design: God has made us *for* Himself.

So what about the other loves? They can be fabulous when your soul is full of the love of God. But they can be devastating when you have expected they could fill up the dry and empty places.

The Man

Hubba, hubba, gotta love that man. A cute guy walks into the room, and, try as we might, most of us girls are momentarily distracted. The swagger. The smile. The strength. The mystique that keeps us trying to figure him out. I'm absolutely sure God planned it that way. There's just something about guys that won't let us go. We are supposed to fall head over heels. We're supposed to give our hearts

God has made us for Himself.

31

away in trust. We're supposed to need their strength. And doggone it, sometimes they can just be cute and funny and handy to have around.

Last week, a friend and I ate in a fabulous restaurant for her birthday. A gorgeous guy with some hunky name like Thad came over to wait on us. He was as charming a man as I've ever met. He told us about the specials while my friend and I gave each other the *hubba, hubba* look across our menus and smiled to each other in girl code. He made our entire meal a delight. Our glasses were never empty. Thad gave all his attention to the details of our lunch, and we were very impressed.

I remember thinking to myself, *Wow, this guy must be a law student or undiscovered musical genius or both. He really has it all going on.* When he brought the check, he hung around, and we began to talk. About two sentences into dialogue that had ventured past lettuce wraps and kung pao scallops, I looked into the eyes of the best-looking man in the room and watched him fade to ugly and gray. I listened as some of the most self-righteous and pompous attitudes I've ever heard came pouring out of him. After he walked away, I said to my friend, "Well, he was cute, until he began to string words together."

Thankfully, it takes more than *hubba, hubba* to capture a girl's heart. Gorgeous catches our eye, but intellect, strength, and compassion can reel us in.

Being reeled in is exciting, and God must certainly delight in the ruckus that goes on when a guy and a girl fall in love. He must enjoy watching the people He created having fun together. A girl who has known healthy love is stronger, more content, and more self-assured. This

> List 5 things that you find attractive in a guy.
>
> 1. _____
> 2. _____
> 3. _____
> 4. _____
> 5. _____

covering of healthy love becomes a safe place to run back to. A haven to rest in. A shelter in the storm. There is someone to come to her rescue. Someone to hold her in the night. Someone to call her beautiful.

It might all be perfect, except that one day we look at the guy who calls us beautiful and decide that he's not enough. Just a few minor adjustments and he'd be a much better complement . . . just a couple of changes and he'd finally get it right. If he'd be on time or fix his front tooth or part his hair differently, maybe then he'd be enough to fill every longing. Maybe he'd make us whole.

Here is one thing I can say with great confidence: the guy that you love is just a man. He may be your soul mate. He is possibly your best friend. He may be hunky and funny and surprising and strong, but he will never—not in a million years, not if he brings you flowers every day and keeps every promise ever written—be enough to fill your soul. He will never make you whole.

He wasn't made to be enough. He could not be even if he tried. He is just a man, and he can give only as a man and interact as a man and love as a man. He wasn't designed to fill the depth of a woman's longings, antici-pate every need, and jump through every hoop.

He can't. Those deep places inside you were made for God. The man is simply a vessel. God uses him to give you a part of the filling of His holy love. But he is not the only vessel, nor is he able to fill you from his own strength, nor is he the only thing you will ever need. Are you hearing this? There will never be a guy on the face of the earth who can make you whole. Being filled in the depths of your soul is only about the love of God . . . knowing Him . . . hearing His voice . . . believing that He's wild about you . . . dancing in His arms.

QUIZ: Is he good for you?

Circle the letter beside the statement that best describes
the relationship with your guy.

1. a. He allows you to be yourself.
    b. He pressures you to please him.
2. a. It's based on trust—words and actions are consistent and honest.
    b. It's based on distrust and fear. You're on guard with him.
3. a. Feelings are shared openly, freely, and spontaneously.
    b. There is an emotional shutdown, a fear of criticism.
4. a. You feel free to ask honestly for what is needed and wanted.
    b. You're playing head games, trying to fish for hidden secrets.
5. a. His interest is focused on you.
    b. You sense uncertainty and that he's just doing things to appease you.
6. a. He welcomes closeness and is willing to risk being vulnerable.
    b. He fears closeness and sees vulnerability as a threat.
7. a. You enjoy being by yourself.
    b. You fear abandonment and loneliness during day-to-day separation.
8. a. He gives and receives unconditionally.
    b. He gives in order to get.
9. a. You and he maintain other friendships and relationships.
    b. You or he neglect other friends and family members.
    a. You don't attempt to change one another.
10. b. You attempt to change one another.

Give your relationship one point for every "a" you circled, zero points for each "b."

If you scored

1–4: Slam on the brakes and run the other way! This relationship is headed for a dead end. In the future, steer clear of the "b" signs. If *you* are the one displaying the warning signs, spend some time discovering why. Then, when you're ready, ask God to show you the way to a healthy relationship.

5–7: Not too bad, but this relationship definitely needs some work. Is this guy worth your time and effort? If so, ask God for wisdom and direction as you try to repair the relationship. Don't pretend that it will fix itself. It won't. And if it doesn't get better after some work, get out.

8–10: Take a minute to thank God for blessing you with a healthy relationship. But don't forget those "b" answers you may have circled. Be sure to get those—and keep those—out of the way.[1]

The guy's responsibility is to be the vessel and to be a good one. He is called to listen to God. To love you in the ways God prompts his heart. If he loves you as a man who walks with God and if you realize that the vessel is just a man, there can be an amazing exchange of healthy love. Through the guy, you can sample a part of the love that God has for you.

A girl's responsibility with a guy is to let him be just that. He is not your girlfriend. He is not perfect, and he never will be. He is not your savior. He is not your filling, nor is he the answer to all your longings. You must let him be fallen and forgiven and in process. You must learn the difference between guys who are healthy and those who are not. You must not mistake his opinions for the opinions of God. He may never call you beautiful or smart or witty. No matter what a guy says or doesn't say, God is *still* wild about you.

You've got to realize that there will never be healthy love between a girl and a guy until the girl comes to rest and find her being in the great love of God. God's love gives wisdom in figuring out the man. God's love gives direction and patience and hope. God's love lets us smile at the guy's quirks, just as God smiles at ours.

I hope that you have heard me. A good guy can be wonderful. But he can never be *enough*, and he can never make you *whole*. You and I were made for even more. We were made for God.

The Other Man

It's impossible to talk about the men in a girl's life without speaking of the other man, the other vessel of God's love—her father. I can be in a small group of women and tell you in a matter of moments which ones have had a healthy, loving relationship with their fathers. There is a certain confidence and peace that comes from a woman who has known such love. And there is an anxiousness and insecurity buried inside a woman who has never known a father's love or, worse, who has suffered wounds from his words or his distance or his hands.

I do not know about the love your dad has given. I just know this: as great as it may have been, it could not be enough to fill you. And if his love was nonexistent . . . if you have known the pain of never pleasing him . . . if you have lived your whole life embarrassed that he was your dad . . . if you have cringed in fear in his presence, there is a Father who wants to heal every wound and wipe away every tear.

No other guy will be able to fill what your father never gave. Nor can any goal or achievement. The only person who can give what you have missed is God. He is the only One who can hold you close enough. He is the only One who can fill where you are empty.

If your daddy never called you beautiful or asked you to dance or swung you around in his arms, you may hesitate when I tell you of God's wild love for you. It's okay to hesitate. You have good reason. But here is where you must push beyond the hesitancy and into the love that waits for you. Believe that God in heaven is not distant. He is not judgmental. He does not reject. He does not harm. I understand that this journey may be difficult. Maybe you shouldn't walk alone. Is there someone who can take you by the hand—a counselor, pastor, or friend—and lead you into the safe arms of God?

Your father was meant to be a vessel. Maybe he has been that. Maybe you have tasted the love of God from the other man in your life. If so, you are blessed. But maybe

He is not judgmental. He does not harm. He does not reject.

he never even came close. Do not lose heart. Remember, he was only supposed to be a vessel. He was one of many. He was never supposed to be enough. You were still made to be filled by God.

Has your father's influence been good or bad, provided strength or weakness? In what ways?

_____

_____

_____

_____

_____

_____

The Friends

I have a best friend who, sadly, lives a whole country away. When we are together, we can look at each other and know what the other is thinking. I know when she is saying with just a look, "Get over here right now and save me from these people." She knows when I am asking, "Is this the dumbest thing you've ever seen?" with only a hint of a smirk. We can show up at an event without having seen each other in six months and have the same haircut.

We crack each other up even when no one else gets it. It's so easy to be with her. I think we're well into ten years of friendship without a cross word or anger or too much disappointment. We are committed to a lifetime of friendship; besides, we've come this far and now sometimes it feels like we would not have made it without each other. I can truly say that her friendship is one of the most consistent, loving relationships I have ever known. She is a vessel of God's love to me, and she is a good one.

But I would be mistaken to ever believe that she could be enough. If I wanted to ruin the blessings we enjoy, all I'd have to do is begin to expect her to fill my soul. She'd feel pressure. I'd be disappointed. We'd grow distant. The whole thing—all the years of our sacrifice to care for each other and the work it takes to build a friendship—would be blown to pieces. She is amazing and lovely, but she cannot be enough. That place is reserved for God.

The Stuff

Because we know that we are empty and filling seems like it would be the answer, we just keep reaching for stuff, hoping it will take up the space in our souls. Shoes, CDs, sunglasses, gadgets—the list is endless.

I don't know what it is about us. Somehow we get to thinking that some new stuff will help us feel better. And it

---

Let's run through some Theology 101 to track the logic of this thinking.

You and I were made—body, soul, and mind—by _ _ _.

We were made for _ _ _.

The part of you that longs to be filled with love is your _ _ _ _.

The soul is empty but can be made whole by _ _ _ _ _ _ _.

There you go. Made by God, for God, with a soul that can be made whole only by His love. These truths are SO important. We can't really go much further until we get this nailed down.

does—for about three seconds. Expecting stuff to fill you up is like holding out the dusty cup of your soul to catch the last drop of water from a broken faucet. It may feel a little wet, but there is nothing else coming to wash away the dust and fill the cup.

Unlike the man, the father, or the friends, the stuff was never intended to be a vessel. Kate Spade, Sony, and DKNY—even in endless supplies—weren't ever intended to add anything to your soul. These things cannot impart to you a taste of the love of God.

Stuff is for necessity and stuff can be a gift to be enjoyed, but the love that makes us whole comes from God. My, how we've gotten things confused. The need for love can never be filled by the pursuit of stuff, and the God of love has promised to provide all the stuff that we need.

Check out Matthew 6:25–34. What exactly does Jesus tell us NOT to worry about?

Our Delight

The attraction to other loves can be a good thing, a very good and beneficial thing. When we get this one right, we have come to understand their purpose. We have come to know the other loves as vessels of God's love for us, and we can treat them with patience and kindness, realizing their limitations, their purpose, and our responsibility.

But when we get this baby turned upside down, we can easily push away from the strong arms of God in search of another love. We can take what was intended for good and make it an idol. We can keep running from relationship to relationship trying to find someone who can kiss like *KA-BOOM* or take us where we've never been or fill the cup of our soul.

The other loves have their places. Sometimes God uses the arms of a guy to hold you. Sometimes He calls on the strength of a father to shape you. Sometimes He calls you on the phone through the voice of your friend to tell you He loves you. They are vessels, all of them, beautiful vessels of His blessing. Each intended for your delight.

Would you enjoy the tastes of God's love that come from the other loves? Think of them as little appetizers intended to make you want more. You have been given an invitation to come and indulge in the feast of God's love. Don't settle for less. Don't stop at the potato skins when there is filet mignon and chocolate cake still to come. Don't expect cheese on a cracker to be enough when a five-course dinner is prepared in the next room. God has so much for you. His love is lavish. His grace is abundant. The invitation is free.

Who would want to miss a love like that?

> Think back for a minute. Who or what have you sought after in hopes of filling the emptiness? How did that turn out? Did you reach the goal only to realize that it wasn't enough?
>
> _____
>
> _____
>
> _____
>
> _____
>
> _____
>
> _____
>
> _____

If there is a question attached to a girl's soul, maybe it's "Do you think I'm beautiful?" When God answers from the depth of His great love, it makes some of us feel like the wallflower who is asked to dance. But we can become distracted from His invitation because of the other loves

and whispers of unbelief.

Chapter 4

Whispers of Unbelief

*B*eautiful? God, I'm struggling here.

I believe that You said it, but did You really mean it about me?

Good grief, You see me in the shower, for heaven's sake.

Beautiful is not the first word that would pop into my head.

Average might be the word I'd use. Common. Ordinary. But not beautiful.

If anyone knows the truth about this body, it's You. Every freckle and flaw and frizzy strand of hair. You witness my attempts to conceal the flaws and curl the frizz. You see me first thing in the morning every single day.

And beyond my body, there is my heart. Again, beautiful doesn't really come to mind here either. Inconsistent. Petty. Insecure. All those words seem to speak the truth that hides inside me.

How could You call me beautiful?

Are You sure? I mean, I know You are God and of course You're sure, but maybe You had some poetic imagery in mind. Maybe You were speaking in broad terms about the beauty of Your creation. Did You really think of me when You said, "The king is enthralled with your beauty"?

I keep hearing these whispers in my head, "Don't believe it, don't believe all of it. Sounds too good to be true. Could be like the guy who said I was beautiful but forgot to call me back. He only meant it in the moment, not for real."

Believing. It seems to be the key to the whole deal with You. I desperately want to believe but unbelief interrupts my effort. Doubts come to me. Skepticism speaks to me. Sometimes I hear what others haven't said about me more loudly than I can hear You. I have believed in You almost all my life, so why does unbelief still whisper to me? Why am I prone to incline my head and listen?

> When I tell you God calls you beautiful, what thoughts immediately pop into your head?
>
> _____
> _____
> _____
> _____
> _____
> _____

The other day, I sat with a counselor for a few hours. I must have voiced some doubts, some hesitation about my value. This guy looked at me and said, "I don't think you know very much about the love of God." Silence. Gulp. I kinda thought I knew a lot about the love of God.

I had been rambling around, talking about my life as if God were saying, "Angela, maybe we ought to sit this one out. Maybe we'll dance again when you pull yourself together." I had been acting like God could not call me beautiful. The result of my unbelief was frailty, weakness, pain, and loneliness. If you want to come undone, just begin listening to the whispers of unbelief about God.

The Whispers

Maybe more than anything, it is unbelief that trips us and keeps us from dancing. Actually, unbelief causes more than a little stumble. It whispers into our souls like a quiet disease and leaves us spiritually crippled and paralyzed. I imagine that if you're reading this book you have some beliefs regarding Jesus as the Son of God. You probably believe that He is who He said He is. You may have asked Him to forgive you of your sins, and maybe you have asked Him to make you His for now and for all eternity. But do you really believe that God, the only One who has the power to save, calls you beautiful? Do you believe that His love for you is truly personal? Do you believe that He will rescue you when you call? Do you believe that He could never turn His back on you? Do you believe that He has amazing plans and purpose for your life?

Maybe no one in this world has ever called you beautiful. Maybe you are overweight or underweight. Maybe you are pear-shaped or tomato-shaped or string-bean-shaped. Maybe your nose is really crooked. Maybe you didn't inherit symmetrical features, high cheekbones, pouty lips, big round eyes, or satin hair. Actually, most of us didn't. Maybe you walk with a limp, roll in a wheelchair, or were born with a physical abnormality. Maybe you look into the mirror and know that a swan is never going to replace the ugly duckling. But we look

> *I do not feel beautiful. I feel unwanted and unloved, and I wonder how God can love me. I know in my head that He does, but the hurt in my heart is so deep that it's difficult to understand being loved like that.*
> —Whitney

into the mirror with *our* eyes. That is the problem. God does not see as we see.

He never has. And we have always tried to rationalize that He thinks and acts like us, but He does not. He is God.

Our thinking has been shaped by taunting, unflattering words from people we love, magazines in waiting rooms, cosmetic counters at the mall, the big screen and the little screen and now the computer screen—all teaching us how to think as the world thinks. I mean, how can we not buy in? After ten or fifteen years of watching and reading and listening, we've really believed this stuff. Essentially,

Start with the good stuff and DO NOT leave this part blank! Write down at least five positive traits about your physical appearance. (Remember the compliments you've received in the past!)	Now for the whispers: write down the frustrations you have in regard to body image. Have people said dumb things about your shape, size, color, etc., that stuck with you? Write them down.
1._____	1._____
2._____	2._____
3._____	3._____
4._____	4._____
5._____	5._____

Go back and read Psalm 45. Who cares about those dumb things people say? What does God call you??? Yup! BEAUTIFUL!!!

we've been brainwashed. Brown hair should be high-lighted. Short statures should wear heels. Chubby figures shouldn't eat.

I have certainly bought into this lie. I rub pink goo around my eyes every night. I don't wear pleats because they puff at the waist. I've spent years in closed-toe shoes because my elementary school friend made fun of my feet. And I know I'm not supposed to think about it, but every once in a while I wonder if I could slip into a plastic surgeon's office and have a few things sculpted, tight-ened, or enhanced without anyone noticing. But isn't that the point—that people would notice? I don't know what the point is exactly, to feel great about myself or to get others to feel great about me. I just know those random thoughts zing through my head from seemingly nowhere.

For heaven's sake, where is it written? Where is it written that what the world calls beautiful is correct? Where is it written in Scripture that God takes instruction from us? Where is it written that man can understand the heart and mind of God? Nowhere. In fact, God makes it very clear that He does not think as we do:

> "For my thoughts are not your thoughts, neither are your ways my ways," declares the LORD.

> "As the heavens are higher than the earth, so my ways are higher than your ways and my thoughts than your thoughts."
>
> Isaiah 55:8–9

Why do we have such a hard time believing that God would look at an ordinary or disfigured girl, call her beautiful, and long for a personal relationship with her?

Maybe we can believe that for someone else, but why can't we believe it for ourselves? Why do we have such a difficult time allowing God's unfailing love to embrace the ugliness of our flaws and the desperateness of our sin? Why do we think that we've gone too far this time, stayed away too long, or paid too great a price to be asked to dance again? The world whispers, "Don't believe it," and we listen. We struggle with unbelief because we have insisted on humanizing God. We have resolved that God must think and process in the same ways we do. Essentially, we have decided that God is not able, when in fact we are the ones who are not.

Clinging to the Whispers

Why do we cling to the whispers of unbelief? I'm going to camp here for a few minutes because I feel these thoughts are life-changing. If we can't get past our unbelief then we will absolutely never know the joy of the dance. We'll continue to live around the edge of life, never truly entering in.

We can resist believing for several reasons.

We've never been close enough to see God work before. It is incredibly difficult to trust someone that you don't know. And if you have only an acquaintance relationship with God, you may not know how trustworthy He is.

Have you ever done a "trust fall"? You are standing on a table, and a bunch of anxious friends from the youth group are behind you, promising to catch you when you allow yourself to fall backward. There is a moment between falling and being caught that makes you wonder if they went for pizza. But when they catch you—whew—what fun to be held and laugh in their arms. It's easier to jump back on the table and do it again because you now have trust.

If you've never fallen back into the arms of God, you don't know the joy of being caught and carried. You haven't seen what He can do with the burdens of your life because you haven't been close enough to allow Him. Maybe you resist Him and struggle with the whispers of unbelief because you just don't know Him and you haven't begun to see how powerful He really is.

We are afraid of what we cannot see. Class schedules. Syllabi. Daily planners. God does not hand out maps and a schedule of events. It's frustrating sometimes, but if we can ever get the hang of life as God intended, then it becomes an adventure to be lived instead of an unknown to be feared. Henry Blackaby says that when you can see, no faith is required. You do not have to be afraid of what you can't see with God. We may need some retraining here, but God will be patient. Lean into Him, and when unbelief whispers to you, lean harder. Leaning is learning how to believe. God is faithful. The dark is unknown only to us, not to Him.

The pride thing. I almost hate to bring it up because we've heard it so many times, but it can't be avoided. Pride will keep us locked in unbelief. It is humbling to give up, put everything down, and then fall into the presence of God. We thought we could make it just fine. We don't like to say we can't. Give me just a little more time or a few more resources, and I can figure anything out. There is the whisper of unbelief: "You can make it on your own." Scripture offers a different view. Jesus said to His disciples,

How would you rate your life with God right now?

❑ Close and intimate

❑ Surface and Sundays only

❑ Distant and rebellious

❑ Some other combination

49

> Are you currently trusting God for anything powerful? Waiting for him to do the impossible? If not, what in your life needs God's powerful helping hand?
>
> _____
>
> _____
>
> _____
>
> _____
>
> _____
>
> _____
>
> _____
>
> _____
>
> _____
>
> _____

"Apart from me you can do nothing" (John 15:5), and then Peter instructed, "Humble yourselves . . . that he may lift you up in due time" (1 Peter 5:6).

One huge step toward greater belief is realizing that you are unable and putting everything down, especially your pride, so that God can pick you up.

We aren't growing up spiritually. Do you look more like Jesus this year than you did last year? How about five years ago? This is what I know about your spiritual life: if you look about the same now as you have for a very long time, then your beliefs about God have not deepened, your trust has not grown, and your faith has not been stretched. I'm not saying that you're shallow; I'm just saying that you're stuck—you are not becoming. The whole idea of belonging to Christ is to look less and less like we used to and more and more like Him.

If you took a spiritual inventory and decided to be gut-level honest with yourself and God, what would the results look like? How would you rate yourself on the growth that is taking place in your soul? Sometimes we are riddled with unbelief because we have stopped growing and becoming.

Learning How to Believe

Here's the deal. You can believe in Jesus Christ as your Savior, make heaven and miss hell, but never realize the power that God intended for you to know in this life. The power that is given to the girl whose life is consumed by the love of God. The power that comes to the girl who believes.

As long as we continue to disbelieve the intimacy and faithfulness of God's love for us, we will live apart from His fullness and complete purpose in us. We may be walking around breathing, but we are not living in strength. Have you spent any time just walking around breathing, taking up space and marking off lists? How did you feel? I'll tell you how I've felt. Miserable. Numb. Fragile. Worthless. Unbelief leaves us empty, powerless, and wandering. Unbelief keeps us living beneath the possibilities that God dreamed for our lives.

God, Help My Unbelief

Maybe you still have doubts. Maybe you hesitate. It's okay. Lean into those doubts and watch what God does. Instead of running from them, pick them up, own them, and decide to lay them at His feet. Some of the most powerful prayer times I have ever had with God were

Unbelief leaves us empty, powerless, and wandering.

times when I came to Him with the whispers of my unbelief. On one of those days my prayer might have sounded something like this:

God, I know You said You would always be enough. Right now it doesn't feel like You are. I find myself searching everywhere to find enough. I am frantic inside. Doubts plague me. Strength eludes me. Where is Your power in my weakness? Where is Your healing? I am embarrassed at my lack of faith. I don't know what else to do except believe anyway. God, help my unbelief. I put my weight down fully. Hold me. Change me. Show me Your glory.

What is so amazing about God is that He really does hold us. He is not put off by our struggles. He does not wag a finger in disdain at our honesty. We can lean into Him with the full weight of our lives. And maybe for the first time in a long time, when you feel God hold you, then doubt and unbelief will begin to fade in His presence. Unbelief becomes belief. Eventually, belief becomes trust. Trust becomes strength and rejoicing.

The world may whisper, "Don't believe it. God doesn't really think you're beautiful." Maybe your life experiences even seem to prove the whispers. Has unbelief held you captive for years? It would be momentous for you to finally believe. Everything would change. What if you began to live as if you believed God's words—all of them? What if you just went for it—staked it all on Jesus, leaned in, gave Him the load you've been carrying, and fell down on top of it? Do you have anything to lose? Nothing.

And to gain? The rest of your life dancing in the arms of God.

God	Satan
• Forgives sin and remembers it no more.	• Spotlights sin and keeps reminding you.
• Wants to clear your path.	• Tries to confuse you.
• Heals wounds and replaces lies with truth.	• Keeps you wounded with repetitive lies.
• Tells you what He has said.	• Tells you what the world says.
• Rewards us with real gifts and blessings.	• Disappoints us with cheap imitations.
• Never stops providing strength for resistance.	• Never stops trying to trip you up.

The Invitation

I have heard the whispers, and yet I am dancing with God. Maybe more intimately than I ever have in my life. I can hear the music, feel the strong arms of my Beloved, sense His gentle leading in every turn, and know that my soul is resting in the assurance of His presence.

I have not come to this intimate dance with God because I memorized Song of Songs or attended three more Bible studies last year or finally got disciplined and began praying every morning at 4:00 a.m. No, I have come to this dance because my world caved in, pretense fell away, every prop I had leaned on broke, and finally there was nothing.

Nothing but God, His music, His unfailing love for me, and the dance . . . this beautiful, intimate dance of trust and grace and mercy. I am overwhelmed to be held in His embrace. Overwhelmed to know that He looks into my eyes and still calls me beautiful. Sad to know that I had been invited all along but missed His nearness because sometimes I had listened to the whispers and turned away.

Dancing with God means that you have chosen to respond to His invitation. He said, "Would you?" And you said, "Of course, I'd love to." It's an act of will. It is an intentional choosing to believe and rest in His strength. It's really your only responsibility. The prerequisite to dancing is answering the invitation . . . choosing God. But we have to keep choosing. The world tries to cut in with unbelief, and we have to decide over and over, do I want to stay right here with God? Will I keep believing?

When the world cuts in and we listen to the whispers, the intimacy is broken. The music is still playing. The invitation from God remains, but we have wandered away from His strong arms. There is distance, distraction, and stumbling. Remember: you and I were made to dance with God. Another partner just won't do. Dancing with someone else will be awkward and embarrassing. We will feel insecure and anxious. We can easily lose our step.

> You and I were made to dance with God.

The Shout

And so what will you do? Will you choose to listen to the whispers? Or will you decide to give up and give in to believing? Lean hard on your decision to believe in God. Put your full weight down. Lie there in His presence and wait for Him to carry you.

The love of God is like an authoritative shout—the final word—that comes to hush the whispers and squelch the rumors. Will you say again today, *I believe. Oh, God, help my unbelief!* Let the truth of God's love be the exclamation that silences the muttering in your head.

He really thinks you are beautiful.

All of you.

Inside and out.

Top to bottom.

Yep, even around back too.

"Beautiful," He says.

If there is a question attached to a girl's soul,

maybe it's "Do you think I'm beautiful?" When

God answers from the depth of His great love, it

makes some of us feel like the wallflower who is

asked to dance. But we can become distracted

from His invitation because of the other loves,

whispers of unbelief,

and noise and clutter.

Chapter 5

Noise and Clutter

About a year ago I was preparing for LASIK eye surgery. My doctor told me I needed to wear glasses for a few months to give my eyes a rest. I had been a severe contact lens abuser, wearing them every waking hour for years. A part of the abuse came from the voices in my head . . . *four eyes, bottle caps, magnifying glasses.* And a part of the abuse was brutal vanity and insecurity. No one had ever given me a second look when I wore glasses, and I had come to believe that I could not be acceptable, much less *attractive*, in them. Wearing contact lenses was for me "doing the best you can with what you have."

I remember first getting my contacts, sitting across from the lady who was teaching me how to properly clean them, put them in, and take them out. We struggled for a while, but I finally got them in. Saline streaming down my face, I looked up at her, beaming with pride. She said, "There you go. Now everyone can see those beautiful eyes you've been hiding." That was enough for me. The lady at the doctor's office liked my eyes, and so I never hid them again. From then on, I rarely let anyone see me in my bottle caps.

Oh, the
stupidity
of vanity!

On a class trip to Europe, I tore a lens on the first day of our trip, but because my insecurity kept me out of glasses, I spent about a week touring the sites blurry-eyed with one lens in and one out. Oh, the stupidity of vanity! I'm embarrassed to even tell you! I got a new lens in Vienna and never did wear the glasses. Needless to say, the first part of my trip—Amsterdam, Brussels, and Munich—remains a fuzzy memory.

Years later, when I was *much* more mature, my eye doctor said, "No contacts for three months," I thought, *Hang on a minute. How can I get out of this one? Do I have to do this? Where can I hide for a quarter of the year?* Then I remembered my glasses back home in the drawer—bent from reading in bed, totally outdated, and missing one earpiece that broke off because it could not be rigged anymore. Vanity raised its ugly head, and I wouldn't even consider wearing them. Dr. Smith gave me a new prescription, and I made a straight path for the mall.

I guess I spent a couple of hours trying on frames and narrowed my choice to two. I sat down with the salesman and took them off and on, imagining how they were going to look with big, thick lenses. I finally asked, "Okay, which one? This one . . . or this one?"

He watched patiently and said with all the enthusiasm of a tired man waiting for a woman to choose eyeglass frames, "They both look fine."

So helpful. *Fine?* I'm thinking, *I don't want fine. I want awesome.*

I tried to prompt him. "Well, these are kind of funky."

"Yep, they're funky," he conceded.

Stuck. He was consistently no encouragement. What was I thinking? Why did I come to choose frames without a girlfriend committee? This could be traumatic. I finally wrestled out some spunk and looked that man square in the eyes and said, "Life's too short. I'm choosing funky."

Obviously moved by my resolve to live adventurously, he said, "Okay, ma'am, they'll be ready in an hour."

I came back later and picked up my funky frames. *Well, maybe I can do this for three months,* I thought. *These aren't so bad. I might even look cute.*

Next, I sought the opinion of a person with the power to encourage or wound. I had no idea what was coming.

"I don't like them."

"Huh? What do you mean? They're fun. They're funky."

"They make you look like you have an attitude. Take them off."

"I can't take them off. I'm blind as a bat without them. Besides, it's only for three months."

"I can't talk to you with those glasses on. You'll have to take them off. I hate them."

Dumbfounded.

Dazed.

Rejected.

I felt so foolish, so alone underneath those frames and thick lenses.

It felt like somebody had just hit me right between my four eyes. *She hates them.* I should have known. I have always looked stupid in glasses. Now I look funky stupid. I can't breathe. This is awful.

That day, I had been screaming, "Do you think I'm beautiful?!?" The voices in my head and the people I

> Sound familiar? I hope not—but then again, I hope I'm not the *only* one who's felt this way. If you've shared my pain, go ahead and write it down. (Then, read on. It gets better. I promise.)
>
> _____
>
> _____
>
> _____
>
> _____
>
> _____
>
> _____

heard made it clear: "No, Angela. Don't you remember? You are not beautiful, especially not *now* in your stupid glasses." The lies I had believed all my life were resurrected with a fury.

It probably took at least two weeks for me to realize that I had to deal with God on this one. Why do we always take so long to go to Him? For days, I had walked around with my shoulders slumped, peering over my glasses, hoping the three months would just evaporate. I finally began to ask, *What is the deal here? Why is this hurting so deeply? Why can't I just get over it? Why does it matter so much?*

God didn't answer me immediately, and as a matter of fact, I didn't realize for a while that He was answering me at all. But something weird began to happen. People began to tell me they liked my glasses. When it became ridiculous, I realized it was God trying to get my attention.

 One day, every single place I went, someone said, "I love your glasses." The lady at the drive-through dry cleaners. The lady at the alterations shop. The bank teller. The post office clerk. It was crazy. People were walking across the dairy section to tell me how much they liked my frames. Total strangers with no reason to say anything polite would come up to me and say, "You look great in those."

Someone even said they were sexy. Lord, have mercy, I

was gushing all over the place, rethinking the whole LASIK thing. And then I realized what was happening—God was answering my cries. He was healing a wound. He was singing gentle love songs over me.

I began to hear God speak to me every time someone complimented the funky frames. It was as if He were saying to me, "You have been lied to, and you believed it. You have listened to all those voices but denied My voice. I think you are beautiful. Let Me exchange My truth for the lies. Let Me quiet the noise, and let Me remove the clutter in your heart. Hear the truth of My adoration. Walk in confidence because of My love."

Noise in your head, clutter in your heart, and distractions for your soul—all are tactics that the world and even Satan use to keep us from dancing with God. They are willing to do anything to make you look away or turn away. They will tell you lies until you believe them. They will play with your head until you give in. They will call your name until you finally answer. They whisper, "Don't believe God," until you can't hear anything else.

Noise and clutter. They infiltrate the mind of a woman, bind up her heart, and hold her life hostage.

> I've been learning lately that God doesn't make us sit in the corner. He holds us while we go through the process of listening for the noise in our lives and dealing with the clutter we've accumulated. I always thought I was going to have to sit in the corner. I'm so relieved.
> —Leigh

Turn It Down in There

"I don't know how to describe it."

"Can you try?"

"It's like there are a lot of voices in my head. It's loud in here. I wish I could turn it down."

"You are not alone. A lot of people tell me it's noisy inside their head."

"Really? This is normal?"

"Yep, perfectly normal, but incredibly distracting."

Is it noisy inside your head? Outside, there's the regular pandemonium: music blaring, phone ringing, everyone talking at the same time. Inside, there's the private noise that no one else hears: *Turn off the curling iron. Dentist appointment tomorrow. E-mail Carla and Jen. Huge exam Friday. Need black shoes for the dance. Need date for the dance! Did I take that book back to the library?*

On and on it goes, lots of tasks and feelings processing in our heads . . . it's the hubbub of life. But that's not the noise I'm talking about.

The noise that keeps us from the dance sounds something like this: *Have I missed something? What was I made for? It's all my fault. Who have I become, and who is the real me? My life doesn't count for much. I'm not sure it's all worth it. My sin is too big. My scars are too painful. I'm an embarrassment. I will never be beautiful. Somebody get me out of here.*

The noise in our head comes from a hundred places—unanswered longings, lies we've believed, fears we've embraced, choices we've made. The noise keeps getting louder through the

If I plugged a speaker into your ear, what noise would I hear in your head? What questions or thoughts bounce around in there?

_____

_____

_____

_____

_____

years, and then one day we can't hear God calling our name anymore. All we can hear are the accusations and the questions and the longings.

We cannot avoid them. We lie down for bed, and they howl through the night. We sit in the bleachers and listen to their conversations about us. The noise will not be silenced. We can't find a switch to turn it off. The problem is that we are not able. Only Jesus can still the soul. Only Jesus can quiet the noise.

The lies about my glasses had followed me all my life and yelled to me through the years. But many other voices had joined in, and eventually there was a ton of junk in my head.

A woman sat with me as I began to process all of this out loud:

"So what do I do with the stuff in my head?"

"I don't know. Let's ask Jesus."

"What you mean?"

"Right now, let's ask Him. Choose one of the loudest voices. What is it saying to you?"

"I'm not sure, maybe the one that says, 'This doesn't make any sense.'"

"Can you remember the first time you heard that?"

"Maybe a few years ago."

"Was there a time before that when you heard, 'This doesn't make sense'?"

"There was a time when I was fourteen. The day my sister drowned."

"Tell Jesus about it. Tell Jesus what you remember."

"Tell Him now?"

"Yes. Tell Him what you're remembering."

I began to ramble, and the tears seemed to overtake

me. Weeping gave way to sobbing. Remembering gave way to reliving. Minutes turned into hours of recounting how this one idea had been shaped in my head.

"Angela, what is Jesus saying?"

"I don't know. What do you mean?"

"What do you think Jesus is trying to say to you right now?"

"I don't think I can hear Him."

"Be still and listen. Look at the scene in your mind. What is He saying?"

Fresh tears. Heart and head pounding from this process.

"I think He's saying that He was with me. But how do I know that it's really Jesus? How can I be sure it's Him and not me making up words I want to hear in my head?"

"It sounds like Him to me. Keep listening."

With the help of a godly woman who guided my prayer with God, I began to untangle the noise in my head. I would hear a voice or words I've heard a million times, and she would direct me to tell Jesus. I'd talk to Jesus while she listened, and then she'd ask, "What is He saying to you?" I'd listen and cry. Question myself and then ask Jesus the question. Laugh and remember. On and on we went, right in the presence of God, handing over each voice, one by one and ugly piece by ugly piece.

When we were done with this extended time of prayer, I was physically exhausted, but my soul was completely quiet. I went directly from this prayer time into a three-day personal retreat of hiking and solitude, where I spent hour upon hour thinking about how an afternoon of intense conversation with Jesus had taken the noise away. I had not been able to still the voices on my own, but in prayer, listening for God's truth, quiet had come like a blanket to cover me.

I don't know what the noise is like in your head, but I imagine from my own journey that you have some (or a lot). The noise is there to distract you, but Jesus wants to take it away. I firmly believe that the noise will never be quieted apart from prayer. You may even need someone to guide you through a day (or many days) of prayer. Expect God to show up. Expect emotion. Expect cleansing. Expect that the noise will finally be stilled in His presence.

Putting Your Stuff Away

You know what clutter is, right? For me, it's the stuff I put on the steps so I'll remember to take it up the next time I go. Then I walk right past it on my way up. I mean to pick it up, but somehow I don't. Eventually, there is another reminder item on the steps, so I run past even more junk the next time. A few more trips up the stairs overlooking the things that need to be put away, and before I know it, there is clutter—a lot of it. And what's worse is, I can get used to looking at it. I know that a pair of rollerblades, three books, and a new bottle of shampoo don't belong on the stairs, but I can still run past them all day long.

In just the same way, clutter comes to our souls. It's the stuff we've climbed over and ignored, thinking we'll get around to it eventually. Soul clutter is the collection of emotional, relational, and spiritual issues we have been stepping over. Each one needs to be picked up, sorted, and put away.

—

Expect God to show up.

—

Clutter can begin to take up so much room in our house that we forget what it looked like clean and orderly. Have you forgotten what it feels like to live without clutter? Have you ever known what it's like to be free of the mess? Soul clutter will keep you from intimacy with God.

I don't know what it is about women, but we'd much rather climb over the clutter of issues than pick each one up and figure out where it came from, to whom it belongs, and where it's supposed to go. Maybe you have fallen asleep right in the presence of God, years have gone by, and now you realize that the Lord is calling your soul to wake up.

Sometimes when we have been asleep spiritually, we wake up to a mess. Sometimes when we wander away from our soul's home, we can return to a disaster. Wherever you've been, no matter how long you've been away, can you commit now to begin dealing with the clutter that takes up space in your soul?

Begin with the Baby Steps

1) Acknowledge the mess. Some of you are neat freaks, and some of you just move the mess around. You know the kind of housecleaning I'm talking about—everything looks great on the surface, but don't open a drawer or closet or look under the bed. It's scary in there.

2) Get messy to get clean. When you acknowledge the clutter in your soul, you also have to realize that you might have to get messy in the cleaning process, and it could take a while to get it all sorted out.

3) Realize that you may have to call for help. I am absolutely the worst at doing this. I would rather throw my back out rotating my queen-size mattress by myself than ask someone to come and help me do it. Don't want to

Types of Soul Clutter

Jot down some personal notes beside any of these that tug at your heart. Be honest with yourself. Then, spend some time in prayer to clean up the clutter in your soul.

✳ Numbing techniques of a hundred varieties

✳ Overscheduling yourself to avoid the emptiness

✳ Gossiping

✳ Isolation

✳ Escaping from reality with movies, books, TV, or the Internet

✳ Lying to yourself or to others

✳ Believing lies you have been told

✳ Rebellion

✳ Rejection

✳ Drivenness and perfectionism

✳ Fears

✳ Envy

✳ Insecurity

✳ Depression

✳ Anger

✳ Bitterness

✳ A critical spirit

✳ Obsessions

✳ Shopping

✳ Body image

✳ Relationships

✳ Lusts—physical and emotional

✳ Self-abuse

✳ Reckless dieting

✳ Sabotaging your health

✳ Addictions

✳ Unforgiveness

✳ Unrepentance—continuing to consciously choose a known sin

inconvenience anyone. Don't want them to hesitate when I ask. Don't want to be needy or helpless or weak. A few months ago, a dear friend worked up her courage and made a difficult phone call. She called to reel me in: "Angela, I know you think that you are strong. Maybe you really are. But if there was ever a time in your life when you needed someone beside you, it would be now. This is not a "stand up and prove you can do it" time. This is a "bear one another's burdens" time. This is a time for people to get on airplanes and come to stand with you. This is the time to ask your friends to hold you up." When my friend called, it was as if my soul breathed a sigh of relief: *I don't have to do this alone. Oh, thank You, God. I don't have to walk alone.*

Asking for help means being vulnerable. It's risky. It's embarrassing. We choose to let someone inside and show them the things we've been hiding. I don't know if you need a good friend, a pastor, or a trained counselor, but I can assure you that the journey should be shared.

4) Pray and seek prayer covering. I truly believe that there will be no power in our lives apart from prayer. We can uncover the mess and begin to walk around in it. We can discuss it and relive the issues. We can wrestle, cry, agonize, and make firm commitments to live differently. But we will not overcome apart from the power of Christ that comes through fervent prayer.

Maybe prayer isn't easy for you. Tell God that. Maybe you feel uncomfortable and don't know what to say. Tell Him that too. The whole idea here is that you turn the gaze of your heart upward. Stop looking to yourself for solutions. Take all of your clutter and lay it at the feet of Jesus.

5) Journal. Words, phrases, diagrams, pictures—anything. Just write where you are. Write about God's guidance. The questions you have. The answers you find. The maturity that happens. The journey is worth remembering. It will be soul-transforming and life-changing. You could be a different person when this is done, and your journal will be the before-and-after snapshots. You will want to remember what God does.

The Eye of the Beholder

Do you remember what the Beholder says of you?

Noise and clutter will burrow themselves between us and the embrace of God. *You look stupid in glasses. You are damaged goods. Your past is too ugly. Your life is broken. You've got a really big mess to clean up. God could never call you beautiful.* We walk around every day listening to that noise.

Is it noisy inside your head? Have you been tripping over the clutter of your life? Maybe it's time to decide to do whatever it takes to be free. Free of the voices. Free of the mess.

Wouldn't it be exciting to believe God instead of the noise? To believe all that matters is the eye of the Beholder?

The One who calls your name is taken with you. The One who knew you before creation is in love with you. To begin to deal with the noise and the clutter is to say, "Hey, turn it down so I can hear the music. Get that stuff out of my way—these feet were made for two-steppin' and I'm here to dance."

> **Why not start now?**
>
> In the box below, write, draw, diagram—whatever—a current snapshot of your soul. Don't be ashamed to include the clutter. It's just going to make your "After" snapshot look that much better!
>
> | Before | After |
> | --- | --- |

If there is a question attached to a girl's soul, maybe it's "Do you think I'm beautiful?" When God answers from the depth of His great love, it makes some of us feel like the wallflower who is asked to dance. But we can become distracted from His invitation because of the other loves, whispers of unbelief, noise and clutter,

and because we are sometimes the prodigal, sometimes the elder brother.

Chapter 6

Sometimes the Prodigal, Sometimes the Elder Brother

I have just returned from the funeral of a prodigal. Rob had everything. Musical talent. Captivating personality. Adoring family. Relationship with God. Beautiful home. Lots of friends. Rob also had an addiction to drugs and alcohol. By the age of thirty-four, he had spent eighteen years taking everything he had, turning toward the distant land, indulging his desires, and then returning with remorse and prayers and resolve. Over and over again, in rehabs, jail cells, and the compassionate arms of his mother, Rob sought forgiveness and fought the demons that hounded his soul. He'd come home sober to parties of Mexican food and jazz music only to be called away again into the darkness of his addiction.

So many tears were cried. So many words were spoken and written. So many prayers were prayed. Eighteen years of crying and pleading and screaming and begging. Eighteen years of hurt and disappointment and mistrust. Eighteen years of wondering when the nightmare would end. And then on Valentine's Day, this prodigal finally went home. He died in his sleep on the couch of a friend after days in yet another binge.

At his funeral everyone knew one thing for certain: even though he had lived too many days in the distant country, teetering back and forth between the strength of truth and the allure of drugs, Rob was without question a child of God, and he was finally home. He was free from the bondage of addictions. The Father had run to meet him and dressed him in the finest robes. The music was playing. The chips and guacamole were plentiful. The party in heaven was a celebration of love and grace and mercy.

I Have Been a Prodigal

I have not made the same choices as Rob, but sometimes I am still the prodigal. I imagine that sometimes you are a prodigal too. Rob knew God. He had heard the music and danced with Him. But there were times when he would choose to leave the strength of God's arms. When the world tries to cut in, I can willfully choose its distraction over the embrace of my Father.

Jesus tells the story of the prodigal like this:

There was a man who had two sons. The younger one said to his father, "Father, give me my share of the estate." So he divided his property between them. Not long after that, the younger son got together all he had, set off for a distant country and there squandered his wealth in wild living.

Luke 15:11–13

Now tell me, who among us hasn't squandered the wealth God has given? How many of us have known better and made a bad choice? How many times have we indulged in thinking or living based on whim instead of wisdom? I am embarrassed to tell you about all my detours, but when I have willfully chosen to turn away from God even though I have known better, I have been a prodigal.

What has the Father given to us? Our share of His estate is the wealth of His grace, mercy, wisdom, and peace. Our riches have come from His great love, patience, forgiveness, and strength poured out to us. There have been times when I have chosen to take His riches and squander them on selfish desire. It's a willful choosing in spite of a "knowing better." Like you, I know the better way. The better way is dancing in the arms of God.

When I remember some past choices, it's like watching a video of myself packing it all up, leaving the dance, and driving off to a place where I am apart from God. I can watch that video now and think, *How stupid was that?* But the girl in the video looks happy. She's excited and curious. She's whistling a tune from the dance. She's too smart to be so naïve. She thinks her life in the distant land will be even better, or that a little adventure will surely be fun.

How many of us have known better and made a bad choice?

Have you ever knowingly left the dance for a visit to the distant country? Have you ever taken everything God has given to you and just left? How would you tell your story of the prodigal?

_____

_____

_____

_____

_____

_____

_____

Life in the Faraway Land

Jesus continues with the story:

After he had spent everything, there was a severe famine in that whole country, and he began to be in need. So he went and hired himself out to a citizen of that country, who sent him to his fields to feed pigs. He longed to fill his stomach with the pods that the pigs were eating, but no one gave him anything.

Luke 15:14–16

When we are in God's presence, we see His riches continually replenished before our very eyes. In His arms, we know the bounty of His lavish love. God keeps giving His goodness, our share of His estate, when you and I are in His presence. But if you have ever packed up your inheritance and driven to the faraway land, you know what happens. The riches come to an end. We spend everything we brought and then begin to be in need. Apart from the presence of God, we become empty and drained of every resource. We go from basking in the wealth God has given to suffering in the poverty of our own choosing. We have been to the dance, but when we leave, we can find ourselves staggering through the mire and muck of pigs. How does a girl find herself spiritually broke and living among swine?

Maybe addictions like Rob's or less dangerous addictions, such as shopping or eating, call her away. Maybe it's the allure of sensual pleasures, obsessions, curiosity about the distant land, or rebellion against the boundaries that have provided safety. Maybe the advantage has gone to the enticements in this holy wrestling match. However it happens, there she is, the daughter of the Father, the girl who used to be rich, now feeding the pigs while her stomach growls and her heart aches for home.

Keep reading what Jesus says:

When he came to his senses, he said, "How many of my father's hired men have food to spare, and here I am starving to death! I will set out and go back to my father and say to him: Father, I have sinned against heaven and against you. I am no longer worthy to be called your son; make me like one of your hired men." So he got up and went to his father.

Luke 15:17–20 (emphasis mine)

I love that the prodigal can come to her senses. We may lose our senses, but our merciful God allows us to return to them. Maybe we have been caught up in foolishness, blinded by whimsy and rebellion. What seemed right wasn't. What felt like fun now feels like cold, slimy mud. But a change of heart can happen in the pigpen. A day can come when the prodigal looks up from the muck and turns her heart toward home. Her thoughts return to her Father and His goodness. That's the day she comes to her senses.

Have you ever returned to your senses? It feels like a veil being lifted, a light being turned on, or a break in the clouds after a foggy journey. When you come to your senses, you wonder where in the world you have been and why it took you so long to come around. If you have ever been a prodigal who came to her senses, you know what I mean. The decisions we make that cause us to squander the riches of the Father are always foolish. No one ever winds up in a pigpen when they have chosen the path of wisdom.

Prodigals Like You and Me

Modern-day prodigals like you and me and the girls we hang out with at church know better than to admit when they've run away with their Father's inheritance. We may be living in a spiritual pigpen, but you can bet we're going to try to camouflage the pit. It's embarrassing to know about prodigals and then become one. Good girls don't make prodigal choices . . . right?

In all likelihood, to admit to another girl that you have been a prodigal only sets you up for more shame, guilt, and labeling. So we vamp up our pretending or work even harder than we already did to perform. It can still look like we're home when in fact our hearts have taken off to the distant country. We know how to speak spiritual words and how to look righteous. Some of us have been going through the motions of appearing holy for a long time anyway.

We can learn to become functional addicts, allowing others to see us as we think we should be seen. Speaking

> **Where would you say you are right now?**
>
> ❑ At the dance, in the arms of God
> ❑ At the dance, standing in the shadows
> ❑ Thinking about taking my inheritance and getting out of here
> ❑ Driving off to the distant country
> ❑ Been living out here in the faraway land for quite some time

out against drinking Sunday morning but then "trying it out" Saturday night. Befriending the new girl at church but ignoring her in front of friends at school. Publicly promising to wait until marriage but pushing the limits with a guy in private. No one is immune to this stuff, but we try to appear to be. We try to hide the choices we've made. We cover as long as we can. We spin the rationalizations in our heads. Just one more time. No one will ever know. I deserve something fun.

And so the distance from home becomes greater. And the heart gets harder. And the riches are squandered. And, eventually, it's unavoidable: every prodigal keeps choosing poorly and spending recklessly until it's all gone. The pleasure is gone. The thrill is gone. Desire is gone. Wealth is gone. She finds herself empty, broke, and hungry, wishing she could go back home and be hired help.

> Can you describe what called or continues to call you away from the dance with God? Addictions? Obsessions? Curiosities?
>
> _____
>
> _____
>
> _____
>
> _____
>
> _____
>
> _____

Watching for Our Return

If the pit of despair is the unavoidable destiny for every prodigal, what is truly amazing and even more certain is that the Father is always watching for our return. We can always go home. We can always return to God.

> But while he was still a long way off, his father saw him and was filled with compassion for him; he ran to his son, threw his arms around him and kissed him.
>
> Luke 15:20

tear-streaked face

weary

physically spent

haggard

hungry

To me, this is one of the most poignant pictures in Scripture. When I think of myself as the prodigal, I see an image of what I must look like spiritually when I have turned away from God: tear-streaked face, obviously hungry and very weary, haggard, and physically spent from the emotion and torment of rebellion. The good girl who made some really stupid choices. The good girl who is so ashamed because she knew better. The prodigal who expects to be condemned and turned away. Besides, isn't that really what prodigals deserve?

When Jesus tells the story, I cry. If I have consciously chosen to turn from my Father and squander the riches of His love for me, it almost seems impossible that when I return, there could be any response except condemnation. Why would He still look for me? Why would He welcome me home? I don't fully understand it, but God watches and waits for prodigals to come to their senses.

Then there is the idea of God running. Not only does He watch expectantly, God runs to us. He sees the repentant heart and the empty hands. He sees His child full of shame over lost riches and stupid choices. He sees the scars of our consequences. And He runs to us anyway. He covers the distance between us with His own strength.

Scooped up into the arms of God. Can you imagine that? Collapsed from exhaustion. Strong arms underneath us. Crying into His shoulders. The sobs that come from shame, the wailing that grieves our choices, and the tears that come from relief. Caressed, kissed, and soothed in the arms of the Father. He brushes the hair from our eyes. He takes our face in His hands. He calms our cries and speaks gentle words over us:

Forgiven.

Redeemed.

Accepted.
Loved.
Beautiful.

Going Home

Have you made some prodigal choices? Do you want to go home? Then make up your mind to turn in that direction. Prodigals go home empty. It's okay. Prodigals go home without options or resources. It's okay. Prodigals go home embarrassed and ashamed. It's still okay. In your returning, you will receive the blessing of God running toward you, His compassion, and His kisses. It is incomprehensible grace to be a prodigal who is held by God again. But read on, there is more:

> The son said to him, "Father, I have sinned against heaven and against you. I am *no longer worthy* to be called your son." But the father said to his servants, "Quick! Bring the best robe and put it on him. Put a ring on his finger and sandals on his feet. Bring the fattened calf and kill it. Let's have a feast and celebrate. For this son of mine was dead and is alive again; he was lost and is found." So they began to celebrate.
>
> Luke 15:21–24 (emphasis mine)

No longer worthy. Since this is a book for girls, we could probably camp on these three words for a hundred years. I have said these words out loud, heard more women lament their worth than I can count, and watched lives stay paralyzed in the land of *no longer worthy.*

Let's just nail something down right now. We are not

79

worthy. We never could be even when we hoped we might. We are not able on our own. We are not good enough and never will be. We are not worthy, never have been, and never even had a shot at trying. That is the whole point. That's the reason we belong to Jesus— because we are not worthy. You may be nodding your head in agreement, but let me ask you a few questions:[1]

Do you feel guilty?

Have you been unable to clean your slate?

Do you feel that you've offended God?

Have you abused others?

Do you carry anger and judgment?

Do you harbor unforgiveness?

Have you looked to false sources of intimacy?

Do you feel shame?

Have you been abused?

Disgraced?

Dishonored?

Humiliated?

Exposed?

Accused?

Spat on?

If you harbor guilt and shame, it's more than likely that you also feel *no longer worthy*. We deem ourselves unworthy to be in God's presence. We don't feel that we deserve to be scooped up into His arms of love. We can't stay there and bask in His joy over us. We can't believe longer than a minute that He thinks we're beautiful. We stay for a moment and then run from Him, dragging our guilt and shame with us. We don't want God to look into our souls. It's heavy and crippling. The embarrassment is almost more than we can take.

The question of your worth has been settled. Did you notice how the father replied to the prodigal's cries of unworthiness?

"Quick! Bring the best robe."

What? Are you sure? Read it again.

"Bring the best robe, a ring, sandals, kill the fattened calf, and let's have a party!"

Do you understand that those are God's words for you too?

Instead of a discussion on dysfunction or a lecture on theology, God says, "Let Me show you how I feel about you. Your worth is settled because you belong to Me." The son belonged to the father. Your value and mine comes from belonging to God, who is saying to the prodigal, "What matters is that you are with Me now. You are home. There is no more shame. No more guilt. All is forgiven. Let's celebrate."

Celebrate. I've met few Christians who do it well. We get together to celebrate and don't quite know what to do. Is it okay to laugh really loud, turn up the music, and dance together because of our great joy? What if we look silly? I'm not sure we know squat about celebration. Where are the "Return of the Prodigal" parties? Where are the "I Was Lost but Now I'm Found" festivals? Heaven forbid we'd look or sound like the heathens, who actually know how to throw a party. Why is it that they have so much more fun? Isn't something askew? Aren't we the ones

Celebrate!

Look around your life and your family. Who needs a victory party soon? Why don't you plan something small (or even large!) in the next few weeks? Cookies, balloons, flowers—anything to celebrate something special. Life is much too short. Dance the happy dance with someone today!

81

with the reason to hire a band, find a strobe light, and throw some snacks out with the punch bowl?

The prodigal cried, "I'm not worthy!" And because worth wasn't even an issue, the father yelled to the help, "Look who's home! Pull out all the stops. Find the best of everything. The one who belongs to me has returned." Belonging was the issue. Belonging was the reason for the party. Belonging to the Father is the reason that we can return as prodigals and receive His great rejoicing over us.

Do you believe that there could be a party waiting for you? You must choose to believe it. Your Father in heaven looks for your return. He runs the distance between you and scoops you up into His arms of forgiveness and love. He celebrates holding you again. He celebrates with music and a dance.

Does that sound like love to you? It sounds like it to me. We might even say that kind of love is blind. God's love for us is not blind, but it feels that way. Because we are covered by the blood of Christ, He is blind to our past. Blind to our squandering. Blind to our lack of worth.

His love is intimate love. Wild-about-you love. When a prodigal turns back toward home, God's wild love runs to hold her.

I Have Been the Elder Brother

Sometimes I have been the prodigal. But more often than not, I have been the elder brother. Believe it or not, being the elder brother can sometimes take us farther from God's heart than being the prodigal.

Take a look at the one who stayed home, the one who didn't rebel or squander his father's riches. The "good" one:

Meanwhile, the older son was in the field. When he came near the house, he heard music and dancing. So he called one of the servants and asked him what was going on. "Your brother has come," he replied, "and your father has killed the fattened calf because he has him back safe and sound."

The older brother became angry and refused to go in. So his father went out and pleaded with him. But he answered his father, "Look! All these years I've been slaving for you and never disobeyed your orders. Yet you never gave me even a young goat so I could celebrate with my friends. But when this son of yours who has squandered your property with prostitutes comes home, you kill the fattened calf for him!"

"My son," the father said, "you are always with me, and everything I have is yours. But we had to celebrate and be glad, because this brother of yours was dead and is alive again; he was lost and is found."

Luke 15:25–32

Have you ever been the "good" one? I have. I've spent most of my life trying to do the right thing. Obviously, in part, it's a firstborn deal, and I am terminally a firstborn. Overachiever. Sickeningly cautious. Working hard to impress. Just wanting everybody to be happy and willing to sacrifice almost anything to make it happen. You know the type. If you're not a firstborn, people like me get on your nerves. If you are a firstborn, you feel a little competition. I'm sure my younger brothers were sick to death of me and my firstborn-ness long before they hit junior high. Craig and J. T. never wanted their teachers to know we were related. They told me, "The teacher would expect too much if they knew you were our sister, so we kept quiet." I'm sure the prodigal felt the same way about his older brother.

All of my trying and the pretense of goodness I have strived for make me well acquainted with the heart and attitudes of the elder brother. There is something inside us elder-brother types that believes if we can just keep all the rules, make wise choices, and live sacrificially, that's it. That's what God requires, and—boom—we're in the club. He must surely approve of our efforts. He must be more pleased with us than those scalawags who come and go. We are as loyal as the day is long. We're proud of our humility and service. We don't quite understand why everyone can't choose as we have.

Gross. Describing my elder-brother tendencies makes me feel queasy. It's uncomfortable when these truths hit so close to home.

Here are some things that I am learning about being a woman who is inclined to be the snotty elder brother: The prodigal knew he was a sinner. *The elder brother could not see his own sinfulness.* At least the prodigal knew what he had done. He had willingly chosen the wrong way but had come to his senses about it. When the elder brother lashed out in judgment and anger, it only highlighted how blind he was to his own sinfulness.

> Do you have eyes to see inside your own heart, or can you just see what's wrong with everyone else? What elder-brother traits do you see in yourself?
>
> _____
> _____
> _____
> _____

Know any controlling, rule-keeping, quick-to-judge types? Then you have known an elder brother. This might begin to get a little too convicting.

The elder brother thought the father loved him because he was hardworking and faithful. The father loved the elder brother all right, but not because of what he did. He loved the older son for the same reason he loved the prodigal son: they both *belonged* to him. It is impossible to face guilt and hidden sin until you reach out empty-handed for the truth of God's love. The elder brother had never stopped working hard long enough to realize what was missing in his life—a joyful receiving of his father's love.

Are you still wrestling with this one? Okay, listen. Your Father in heaven is crazy about you. No matter if you're a prodigal daughter or an elder-brother type, the reason He loves you is the same: because you belong to Him. This has nothing to do with what you do, have done, or will do. I know; it never really makes sense in our little brains, but it's still true just the same.

Because the elder brother had not known grace, he was not able to extend grace. The elder brother could not give grace to the prodigal because he had not known the grace that was present in his father. When you live all your life believing that love comes by works, then that is the basis on which you give love. When you have never believed that the Father sees you and calls you beautiful just because you belong to Him, then you are not able to extend that same free acceptance and mercy. Life becomes bondage to works and moral living. It's ironic that the elder brother thinks he knows so much, because he knows nothing about the life of freedom that comes with the father's love.

When I run into a woman who knows something about grace, I stop and try to take her in. She is rare and worth knowing. Always, always, always I find that a woman of grace and tenderness has become so because she has received an overwhelming grace from God. You cannot extend what you have not known. You cannot impart what you do not possess.

The elder brother was bound by unforgiveness. Forgiveness begets forgiveness. Deep calls unto deep. The elder brother could not forgive because he did not realize how much he had already been forgiven by his father.

You and I will never be asked to forgive someone more than we have already been forgiven by God. Kind of puts it all in perspective, don't you think?

The elder brother didn't know that he had always possessed the riches of the father. It's interesting that the elder brother had lived with the father all that time but had never gotten to know him. When you are with the Father, you are a partaker in all His wealth. The elder brother had been in his father's presence the whole time, yet he had not realized that the family treasures were his to enjoy.

How often have we been in the presence of God and missed the gifts that He had for us?

The elder brother didn't hear the music with his heart. He didn't know he'd been invited to the dance. He could hear the sounds, but to him they were dissonant. How could there be music and dancing for a prodigal? The elder brother was haughty. He was only thinking of himself. His heart was hard in contrast to the tenderness of the father. And because his spirit had been shut down by anger, he was deaf to the music and the dance. He completely missed the celebration of his father's grace.

How many times have I missed the music and the dance because of judgment or self-righteousness? How many times have I denied grace to someone, deciding they deserved judgment more? How many times have I been unforgiving though my Father has forgiven me much? "How many times?" is a scary question. I don't think I could stand to know the answer.

The Way of the Elder Brother

How about you? When have you been the elder brother? When have you held on to self-righteous attitudes and legalism? When have you forsaken the Spirit and heart of the Father because you chose the letter of the law instead? When have you whined and secretly harbored resentment when someone else was covered by the grace of God? Have you ever thought to yourself, *Hey, wait a minute; she's getting off too easily?*

Okay, fess up. You've been there too, right? Spill it. And don't worry—God forgives the elder brother too.

_____

_____

_____

_____

_____

_____

_____

_____

_____

The elder brother is really an insecure guy. He's smug and full of pretense. He is plagued with fears and probably hauling around a cartload of pain. He feels like the victim and wonders why the prodigal seems to be getting a break while he stayed home and can't seem to get anywhere.

When I am the elder brother, my intimacy with God is hindered by my attitudes and judgmental spirit. But if I keep peeling back the layers, I find that underneath my self-righteousness is a woman fueled by fear, pain, and sorrow.[2]

The "elder brother" works so hard because she fears:

- Rejection

- Betrayal

- Exposure

- Being alone

- Pain

- Insecurities

- Consequences of sin

Go ahead and circle any that apply to you. Jot down thoughts about each one you circled.

_____

_____

_____

_____

_____

_____

When we manage our lives around fear, we don't fully trust the motives of the Father. How can you put your weight down and lean into God when you don't completely trust Him? When He asks you to wait, you'll feel afraid. When He asks you to suffer, you'll doubt His heart of compassion.

Pain and sorrow begin to stir up anger inside us, and then we feel some sense of entitlement with God over our sufferings, as if He owes us something for all the pain we've had to endure. Instead of allowing the pain in our lives to shape our character, taking us through the rivers of humility and brokenness, we can let the sorrow become overwhelming, choking out life, filling us instead with bitterness and resentment.

The elder brother has an attitude. He's mad. His heart of judgment is fueled by pain and insecurity. When I have been the elder brother, oh, how my heart ached under the weight of such great animosity.

What's a Prodigal/Elder-Brother Kind of Girl to Do?

When I was a prodigal, I missed the dance with God by my own choosing. I ran away or hid away in the shadows, clutching my guilt and shame.

When I was the elder brother, I didn't even hear the music. Laden with fear, pain, and sorrow, I chose my own haughtiness over grace.

So, what's a girl to do? How do I get back to the arms of God? I don't want to spend any more time away from the dance. It's lonely out there in the distant country. My life is empty and miserable when I'm all tied up with rules. When the world tries to cut in, I need the most direct route back to God.

Over and over again, the answer will be the grace of

God and the already finished work of Jesus on the cross. Remember what Isaiah said about Him?

> But he was pierced for our transgressions, he was crushed for our iniquities; the punishment that brought us peace was upon him, and by his wounds we are healed.

Isaiah 53:5

The sins belong to us, and yet Jesus bore them in our place. Whether we have sinned or sin has been done to us, God still paid the price for all of it. Jesus' death on the cross has paid for my sin and my heartache. His work on the cross is the reason for celebration. We belong to Him, and because of our place in His family, debts are relieved and the riches are shared.

Whether you find yourself as the prodigal or the elder brother, the answer is the same. Take everything that keeps you from His arms to the cross and leave it there. Think about where you struggle and the issues that cause you pain. Take them to God by way of prayer. And keep taking them there until they are no longer yours. They have been paid for in full. Only the blood of Christ is enough to cover the pain and ugliness of your suffering. The strength to finally be free from your bondage is there. Paul said that "it is for freedom that Christ has set us free" (Galatians 5:1). You cannot dance in the arms of God still shackled to the chains of your sin and pain.

Whispers of unbelief. Noise in our heads. Clutter in our souls. The choices of the prodigal. The sins of the elder brother. The world tries to cut in and distance us from the arms of God. Surrounded by the fires of our choices, we are helpless. We will surely burn if left to our own devices. We cannot save ourselves.

Grace is the hand of God that reaches into the fire and rescues us from above. Grace is the forgiveness and mercy that have come to us because we belong to Jesus. Grace keeps asking us to dance. Grace is the reason that a girl like me and a girl like you can hold up our heads and return to the Father.

Grace is having been the prodigal or the elder brother who is coming home empty-handed, surprised to find that God runs, scoops you up into His arms, looks into your eyes, and still calls you beautiful.

Grace keeps asking us to dance.

If there is a question attached to a girl's soul, maybe it's "Do you think I'm beautiful?" When God answers from the depth of His great love, it makes some of us feel like the wallflower who is asked to dance. But we can become distracted from His invitation because of the other loves, whispers of unbelief, noise and clutter, and because we are sometimes the prodigal, sometimes the elder brother.

To return to the music and strong embrace of God requires a desperate and pursuing heart.

Chapter 7

A Desperate and Pursuing Heart

I'm not sure that I have ever been desperate for anything. I've been hungry, but never really starving one time in my whole life. Poor, but never without the ability or opportunity to earn. I've been tired, and that may be as close as I've ever been to being desperate.

It seems like desperate has to do with extremes. Extreme need or extreme measures or extreme desire. Going beyond what one would ordinarily deal with or long for. And my whole life, I have avoided extremes. I am a middle-of-the-road kind of girl. Safe. Observant. I work my way into the pool a few inches at a time . . . no diving into ice water for me.

I don't think I really know what it means to run after something as if your whole life depends on it. When I think about it, I'm not sure I know a thing about passionate pursuit—I work hard and try to stay focused in the same direction, but *passionate pursuit?* Have I ever really been there in my lifetime? Maybe more importantly, have I been called to a life of desperate passion and missed it? Settled for mediocre passion instead?

As my life has unfolded over the past few years, I am finding myself desperate. Desperately ready to know more of God and the depths of His love. Desperately longing to live in the center of His grace and mercy, learning to run after Him as if my whole life depends on it.

If there is a question that I hear over and over when I speak to women, it is, "How do I get to God?" The question may be cloaked in a hundred ways, but the heart of each woman is the same: "I want a passionate relationship with God. I want the romance. I want to dance. I want to believe that He's taken with me. But how do I get there? And then, if I get there, how do I stay?"

So many of us nod our heads in agreement; we want God. We believe the truths of Scripture and the claims of Christ, but we can't seem to find the passionate life with Him. We have settled for mediocre. We're tired of standing around the edge of our lives watching. We want to jump into the middle of the room, but something holds us back.

By now, you may be saying to yourself, *I believe that God calls me beautiful. I know that He sees me and invites me to dance. I realize where the world has tried to cut in. But I'm still not sure how to fully get there. I want to dance, really. I don't want to pretend the romance or read about it anymore. I want to live it. I want to know that kind of strength and live from confidence. I'm willing to be desperate and extreme. Just tell me how.*

Churchy Girls

For most of my Jesus days, I have been a churchy girl. You know girls like me—we're everywhere. We smile a lot. We serve a lot. We volunteer and bake cookies and show up for prayer meetings. It's fun to be a churchy girl because it's like a little club. There is a lingo and rites of passage, and who knows, there may even be a secret handshake somewhere.

Once you get this churchy-girl thing down, it feels like you have God figured out too. You know what's coming at the Bible study or the midweek prayer meeting. You know all the books of the Bible in order and can find Habakkuk without batting an eye. You know the appropriate times to smile, to nod your head in agreement, to murmur an amen, or to raise your hands in worship.

I'm in church:

❑   Every time the door is open (Oh, wait—I have my own key. . . .)

❑   Sundays and Wednesday nights

❑   Sunday mornings (especially when they're serving donuts in Sunday School)

❑   Every Easter and Christmas

You kind of get this whole church groove going, and it begins to feel like you've made it somehow. Bible study once a week. Wednesday night dinner. Outreach projects. Youth group retreats and fundraisers for the pregnancy center. And let us never forget the crème de la crème for all churchy girls . . . Vacation Bible School. Whew. The churchy girl is busy, but that means she's really close to God, right?

You just keep going to retreats and listening to the same dull stuff, hoping something new and radical will pop up. Maybe you've done so many Bible studies and listened to so many sermon tapes that you've almost decided there is nothing new under the sun. Maybe you're

Where is the passion?!

tired of serving. Tired of smiling. And tired of prayer requests about Aunt Margie's cousin's wife's ingrown toenail. Maybe you have become a proper churchy girl. Biblically educated. Hospitable. Quiet and gentle. But for some of us, incredibly empty.

Where is the passion, for heaven's sake? Where is the dance? Would somebody please turn up the music? Maybe we're missing something. We're hanging out at church, being faithful to pray and read the Bible, confessing and repenting. So why aren't more of us working in strength? Why are so many of us dying on the inside, longing to be known as beautiful, suffering underneath the weight of guilt and pain? Why are we sad and hesitant and afraid?

Besides, who can you tell? Try sharing that little nugget of your struggle during closing prayer requests at the girls' group and then look up into their distantly sympathetic eyes. All of a sudden, what was meant to be honesty for the sake of accountability seems stupid. You wish you could take it all back. It feels like you have cooties. Worse yet, wait until someone thinks that she can fix your emptiness or sadness or stronghold or sin with a spiritual cure-all for what ails you, all done in the name of Jesus, of course. There will be prayers and hugs but rarely will anyone else be willing to admit that her soul is as dry as dirt too. Or that she struggles with sin. Or that she feels insecure and lonely.

A part of me understands. We've all been burned. We have shared private details of our lives only to find out later that our heartaches have been e-mailed to forty-six others around the country. Someone speaks to you at school, and then you realize they know something you had shared in privacy. And so we pull back. We decide not to allow ourselves to be vulnerable. We want to trust the body of Christ, but we still smell like smoke from the last time. Most of us know this pain too well.

So we don't tell. We just keep smiling and serving and wondering when we're going to become as spiritual as the women we compare ourselves to. We think that if we could just break free from bondage, if we could just become more disciplined, if we could just overcome our frailty and humanness, we might get to dance. Then we might taste passion with God. We beat ourselves up and remain isolated in the pain of believing that no one shares this journey.

But this is not how it should be. And by some means, it has to change. Maybe it can begin with you and me. A few of us willing to be honest with our struggles and bear the consequences of telling the truth. A few of us willing to risk it for the sake of greater passion and deeper grace. A few of us willing to bare our souls and then openly beg for the grace and mercy of Jesus. It would be a life-changing ministry if we began to pursue Christ with such candor and desire. Real ministry happens in the presence of vulnerability and transparency.

> What, if anything, are you currently doing that could be labeled "churchy girl"?
>
> _____
>
> _____
>
> _____
>
> _____
>
> _____

I'm not saying that we're all pretenders. It's just that so many of us in the Christian community have chosen churchy-girl pretending over a passionate, vulnerable, desperate pursuit of Christ.

I guess this is the place where I need to share something more about my own lousy disguise. I have been a churchy girl and *liked* it. Knowing what to say or pray at the right times has felt safe. Smiling politely kept everyone at arm's length. I have come home from church filled with fresh words from God and yet believing that I must disappoint Him miserably. I have beat myself up over my lack of discipline. I have felt my own pretending at times and it made me sick, knowing that on the inside there was a frantic little girl, lost and trying to find her way home.

Maturity in Christ has to do with understanding the depths of God's grace and forgiveness. Maturity in Christ is about consistent pursuit in spite of the attacks and setbacks. Maturity in Christ is not about finally attaining some level of pseudo-perfection. It is about remaining in the arms of God. Abiding and staying, even in my weakness, even in my failure.

Unchurchy Girls

As is true with almost everything, I don't usually get it until I see it or feel it or touch it. About sixteen years ago, God led me to a woman of grace and mercy and unparalleled transparency. She was an unchurchy girl, and I fell in love.

Do you remember the prodigal named Rob from a few chapters ago? My unchurchy girl is Rob's mom, Carlye Arnold, and this is how God introduced us.

I was in seminary in Dallas and interning with the student ministry at a church in Arlington. Carlye's other son, Dace, was in the eighth grade, and he went home and told his mom about this girl who worked at the church. He thought they needed to get to know me and have me over to housesit. When Carlye tells the story, she says that she didn't want to get to know me. Her life was full of people and plenty to do, but she indulged her son and came by the office. She asked me to housesit, and afterward their family would let me spend the night in their home to avoid the long drive back to Dallas. Over the next year, Carlye and her husband, Jerry, began to call me their daughter. Their guest room was my room, and our love for one another grew.

When I met the Arnolds, their oldest son, Rob, had already been using drugs for several years. But what surprised me was that it wasn't a secret. The whole church knew and prayed consistently for their family. The neighbors knew. The youth group knew. There were other families in the church who had the exact same problems with addicted children, but they chose to be silent and suffer alone. Caryle said she couldn't. The strength to face each new battle came from telling the truth and being held up in prayer. She wasn't trying to suffer alone to prove she was spiritual or godly. She and Jerry suffered openly and without shading the truth.

I remember being in a department store dressing room while Carlye was outside the door waiting for me. I listened to her tell a couple of sales clerks that Rob was addicted to drugs. I was pulling a shirt over my head thinking, *Who in the world are you talking to? Do you know those people? Don't tell them that.* Drawn in by Carlye's gracious honesty, one of the women, in turn, opened her heart and shared a similar burden. Before we left, each had committed to pray for the other. God had been present. The kind of stuff that matters had happened. And me? The one who has always been afraid to be real? New shirt. Same old churchy girl inside.

You have to understand how foreign this transparency was to me. I had wrangled myself into being very careful to maintain a lofty, churchy-girl appearance. I had never met a godly woman who came without bags of spiritual pretension. Carlye was in love with Jesus, but she was so unchurchy. Refreshing. Disarming. Thankfully, very real and unaffected by lingo and pretending. She was honest about her struggles and shortcomings.

Because of her heartache over Rob, Carlye was left without judgment and full of compassion for people who struggle in sin and the families who find their hearts broken.

I have learned more about the real grace of Jesus from hanging out with Carlye than I ever have from words on a page or lectures in a room. It's all these years later, and I am still their daughter. We talk on the phone about twice a week. People say that you don't know how dry you are until you get around somebody who's wet. I have been one dried-up sponge of a girl, a Pharisee, a legalist, a pretender, but Carlye continues to slosh out the freedom of grace all over me and everyone who gets in her path.

Some of the gifts of our friendship have been the life-altering lessons of honesty and openness and the life-giving studies on grace and love. Not one word has ever been taught from a workbook or an outline. Carlye has lived these lessons before me so that I could feel and taste and see the goodness of God in the land of the living.

From churchy girl into the freedom of honesty and

> I'm doing the churchy-girl thing because I don't want to be desperate. I have become fine with serving and working because I'm afraid of the deeper places.
> —Lauren

desperate pursuit. It has been a scary journey for me. But I finally came to realize that I was never going to get to the heart of God by staying inside the lines I had drawn around my life. The life I longed for was on the other side of what had made me feel safe. I wanted the arms of God and not the safety of the shadows. The question in front of me was figuring out how to get there.

Poor in Spirit

Some of us may have to lay aside our churchy-girl pretense in order to stand before God as the unchurchy girl, raw and without excuse. Dancing with God requires vulnerability and a true assessment of where we stand, the resources we have, and the struggles we face. We have to be able to honestly look into our lives and see the clutter. We have to be willing to admit where we've turned away from God or been lured away. We have to look at our lives and own up to the places we've fallen short.

I'm going to assume that you believe the Bible is true. I'm staking my whole life on it. So that's where we're going to look for the answers. If we will keep returning to the words God wrote for us, honestly bringing our lives before their truth, we will find every direction needed for remaining in His arms at the dance.

To be in the arms of God is to be experiencing the kingdom of heaven right in the middle of your real life. And so the question that clamors for an answer is, "How do I get into the presence of God and stay there all of my days?"

In Matthew 10:7, Jesus instructed His disciples to tell people that "the kingdom of heaven is near." That means ordinary folks like you and me could know the very presence of God in their daily lives through His Son, Jesus Christ.

Because of Jesus, people could know the power of healing and deliverance from sin and sorrow. He was saying that when we are in His presence, all of God's riches are available to us, and that means the kingdom of heaven is a lot closer than we realize.

A little earlier, Jesus spoke to some people who had followed Him to a mountainside. Here is the first blessing that He gave to them that day: "Blessed are the poor in spirit, for theirs is the kingdom of heaven" (Matthew 5:3).

The kingdom of heaven. That's where God the Father keeps His wealth and treasure. The kingdom of heaven is where we find grace and mercy. The kingdom of heaven is where hearts get mended and bodies get healed. The kingdom of heaven is where we dance in the arms of our Beloved. My heart longs for the peace and stillness of heaven being near. I want Jesus to take me by the hand and walk me right into the presence of God . . . the kingdom of heaven. I want to be as close as I can get to God on this earth. Jesus says that that place—the arms of God, the presence of God, His nearness to us, *the kingdom*—is a blessing that comes to the poor in spirit.

Blessed means that you and I have been approved by God. He is pleased. We are acting in a way that gives Him honor. We have truly found His heart in a matter. I deeply desire God's blessing.

Sometimes in the Bible *poor* means "without funds" or "without the ability to acquire goods." Sometimes it means "poor for a season," like, "I'm poor this week, but I'll be okay once I get paid." In this case, when Jesus said *poor,* He meant utterly destitute, poverty-stricken, helpless. And so Jesus is saying that God approves of those who know poverty of spirit, and He gives to them the fullness of His presence.

But what is this "poverty of spirit"? What does it mean to be utterly destitute? It means that we are wholly needy, flat-broke beggars with no resources available. It means that you and I have been honest with God and come to realize that we are without an ounce of hope if left to our own designs. This is desperate poverty.

When we have been completely vulnerable with God, we can admit that we have no assets to cling to. We don't have a stash that will get us through. There are no favors to call in. We don't have power or prestige or influence. We will surely starve to death if left to our own means. When there is real poverty in your soul, there is desperation.

Picture in your mind the scene of starving people in a Third-World country. Children are dying with swollen bellies from malnutrition. Disease is rampant. Day after day, the only task, the only important thing, is finding something to eat or drink. The people are desperate and without any resources of their own.

One day the trucks from a relief organization arrive with fresh water and bags of grain. How do the people respond? Do they stand politely in line with their cup for water and their bucket for grain? Do they politely ask, "May I have some water if it's not too much trouble or if there's any left?" No way. These people are desperate. They are starving. They are hopeless without the supplies. And so they charge the grain truck. They climb over one another to get to the food that will save them. No one who is starving is polite and orderly. When you are starving, you are desperate.[1]

Real poverty is not polite. It is determined to get the object of its need by whatever means necessary. When there is real poverty, there is desperation, and we cry out to be fed or we will surely die.

Real poverty is not polite.

God says that's what it means to be poor in spirit. So desperate that we charge the grain truck. So hungry for Him that we'll do anything to get to Him. God says that He approves of those who have that kind of desperation. He gives to them the kingdom of heaven, the fullness of His riches, the peace of His presence, and a hope for the future.

And so how do we get to God? Jesus says to charge the grain truck. Take an honest look at your starving belly and realize that you cannot feed yourself. Do not stand politely in line and wait for some grain to fall to the ground. Use every means necessary to go after the only thing that will save you. Let the pain of your hunger and the truth of your circumstances force you to climb over every obstacle that stands between you and the grain that awaits you in God.

Look around and see if anyone is willing to charge the grain truck with you. There is so much more strength when we band together. Who will charge with you?
How will you begin?

_____

_____

_____

_____

_____

_____

_____

Eat, Sleep, Drink, Breathe

I know this may sound radical to you, but I don't believe that charging the grain truck is supposed to be a once-or-twice-in-your-life event. I believe that we are supposed to live in that poverty of spirit, in extreme desire, until it becomes a life of desperation for God. Desperate enough to run toward Him as though our whole life depends on it.

Being desperate for God keeps us wrapped in His arms at the dance. Being desperate for God has meant for me that I am learning to eat, sleep, drink, and breathe Jesus, climbing over anything that keeps me from Him. I realize that it sounds extreme. It sounds like nothing else I've ever done in my life, but I don't know of any other way.

To eat, sleep, drink, and breathe Jesus means that I am learning to give priority to the pursuit. It does not mean that I am superspiritual or anywhere close to arriving. It just means that I am dragging myself into His presence and staying there. It means that I am choosing not to run away from God even in the shame of my sin. I am crying into His shoulder instead of numbing the pain of my life. I have stopped looking everywhere else to be filled and realize that He is the only One who is able. I am putting His Word into my mind even when I am empty or useless or mad. I am laying down the churchy-girl pretense and becoming a desperate unchurchy girl.

The world tries to beat me away from the grain truck. To eat, sleep, drink, and breathe Jesus is to keep fighting, keep running, and keep charging after the only thing that will feed my soul.

> "The Lord your God is with you,
> he is mighty to save.
> He will take great delight in you,
> he will quiet you with his love,
> he will rejoice over you with singing."
> Zephaniah 3:17

It means that you keep coming back to prayer even when you cannot see one answer. Keep reading the words in the Bible until the Holy Spirit shows up and gives you understanding. Keep hanging around other believers even when they have disappointed and caused pain. Keep bringing every ugly thought back into captivity. Keep repenting even if you're tired of repenting. Keep singing the praise of worship even when your heart seems to be dying.

Remaining desperate.

Remembering that we cannot do it on our own.

You and I are utterly destitute and starving to death without God.

His Great Delight

What does God do with a desperate girl? I imagine that He smiles as He lifts her up into His presence.

God delights in the desperate heart that keeps charging the grain truck for food. He delights in the vulnerability that leads us to the end of our rope. But why would God delight in a girl who is without resources and without any hope in herself?

Only because of Jesus.

Because of His love for us, God sent His only Son to pay for every frivolous choice and every blatant sin and every dead-end path we have taken. The book of Romans says that God treated Jesus as a sinner so that He can now treat us as righteous. It's almost unbelievable that because of Jesus' punishment, we can receive God's great affection. Because of Christ's obedience, we are the objects of God's great delight.

My friend Scotty Smith says, "This is the heart of the good news, the gospel: Jesus has been punished for our sins so that the floodgate of God's affection can be loosed on us like a healing river! He died that we might dance."[2]

And dance we shall!

When a girl gets desperate for the presence of God, He comes in His great love to rescue the one that He adores. He takes her into His arms and quiets every fear. He gives her the grain that feeds her emptiness. He puts a hand over her mouth when she begins to claim she's not worthy.

And then He sings.

I picture the dance and being held close and God whispering into my ear His songs of love.

Wow. I am swooning.

When I come in complete dependence, clamoring, desperate, and empty, God picks me up, holds me, and sings gentle love songs over me. He looks into my soul and sees the question. Before I can even ask it, He tells me that He thinks I am beautiful. He feeds my starving soul with the food of His love. Hear Eugene Peterson paraphrase the passage in Psalm 45:

Now listen, daughter, don't miss a word:
forget your country, put your home behind you.

Be here—*the king is wild for you.*
Since he's your lord, adore him.

10–11, THE MESSAGE (emphasis mine)

I promise I am not making this stuff up. You may have skipped over the books of Zephaniah, Song of Songs, and this passage in Psalms, but don't miss it now. It is so amazingly good and even more true: the King is wild about you!

Yep, I know, still kind of hard to believe. . . . He's really talking to you and to me.

Near the Kingdom

Now in all this excitement, did you hear the answer to the question, "*How do I get to God?*"

Maybe you are somewhat like me, and the first step toward the answer is to begin laying down churchy-girl pretending. Actually, it'll lighten your load by a ton! Whew. Wish I'd known that a long time ago. As a side note, only pick something back up if God tells you to. God will speak directly into your heart and mind and let you know . . . He rarely speaks to us through committees. Let Him direct every step toward reclaiming your heart.

Now that you've laid down the stuff, go ahead and look inside your soul. Anything powerful in there? Anything holy? Anything good? Probably not. There is a want-to. There is a desire. But there is nothing inside me that can make me whole.

So go ahead and admit it. Empty. Starving, actually. Desperately hungry and dying to have food that will last. I have tried, but I cannot feed myself. I am without resources. I am incredibly poor.

There . . . we're almost at the answer. The girl who realizes that she cannot fill her own soul and becomes desperate for God to save her . . . the girl who decides to do anything to get to God: charge the grain truck, climb over every physical and emotional obstacle, begin to eat, sleep, drink, and breathe Jesus . . . that girl is kneeling near the kingdom of heaven . . . that girl is in His arms . . . held and secure and loved.

Look inside your soul. ▼

▶

108

That girl is dancing while God sings gentle love songs.
Oh, God, make me an unchurchy girl.
Make me desperate.
Make me Yours.

If there is a question attached to a girl's soul,

maybe it's "Do you think I'm beautiful?" When

God answers from the depth of His great love, it

makes some of us feel like the wallflower who is

asked to dance. But we can become distracted

from His invitation because of the other loves,

whispers of unbelief, noise and clutter, and because

we are sometimes the prodigal, sometimes the elder

brother. To return to the music and strong embrace

of God requires a desperate and pursuing heart.

And when a girl chooses to remain in

His arms of devotion,

God gives the only hope we have.

Chapter 8

The Only Hope We Have

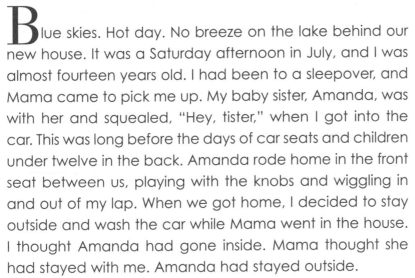

Blue skies. Hot day. No breeze on the lake behind our new house. It was a Saturday afternoon in July, and I was almost fourteen years old. I had been to a sleepover, and Mama came to pick me up. My baby sister, Amanda, was with her and squealed, "Hey, tister," when I got into the car. This was long before the days of car seats and children under twelve in the back. Amanda rode home in the front seat between us, playing with the knobs and wiggling in and out of my lap. When we got home, I decided to stay outside and wash the car while Mama went in the house. I thought Amanda had gone inside. Mama thought she had stayed with me. Amanda had stayed outside.

After only a few minutes, Mama called out to me, "Where's Amanda?"

"I thought she was inside with you."

"She's not here. See if you can find her."

In the next moment, I spotted Amanda. She was floating facedown beside the pier behind our house. I screamed for Mama and ran to get her out. I can still remember almost every detail of stepping down into the water onto a stone and then into the mud, my shoes filling with water, my jean shorts trimmed in peach and the peach-colored shirt that matched, my mom standing on the bank with her hands outstretched. It seemed like I moved in slow motion to put Amanda into her arms. Mama is a nurse, and she began CPR immediately while I ran for help.

I called the paramedics and then called my dad. I cannot even imagine what it sounded like to him when I said, "Daddy, come home. Amanda has drowned."

Most of our neighbors were out of town, and the boats on the lake all seemed to ignore my frantic screams and waves. Finally a lady across the street heard me and yelled, "Honey, is everything okay?"

"No—hurry, we need help! Hurry!"

She ran to me at the pier, and we watched in complete helplessness as my mom valiantly used every lifesaving skill she knew to save her daughter's life. Amanda coughed out some water, and I had hope. Mama worked so hard and begged her baby to hang on.

Almost instantly, our yard was filled with cars, fire trucks, paramedics, my dad, my brothers, friends, and people I'd never seen in my life. They made us step back to watch from the grass, and on that hill behind the pier, my young teenage soul came undone. I was wailing and crying out to God, but this church kid didn't know how to pray. And so I prayed the only thing I knew. I yelled the Lord's Prayer over and over.

Our Father, who art in heaven, hallowed be Thy name. Thy kingdom come. Thy will be done on

earth, as it is in heaven. Give us this day our daily bread. And forgive us our trespasses, as we forgive those who trespass against us. Lead us not into temptation, but deliver us from evil, for thine is the kingdom and the power and the glory forever and ever. Amen.

Our Father, who art in heaven, hallowed be Thy name. . . .

Again and again, I sobbed through these Bible words, demanding that God hear the real prayer in my heart, the one I didn't know how to pray: "God, please save my sister!"

God didn't save Amanda that day.

My mom had done everything right. The paramedics took over and intensified the effort, but her life could not be reclaimed. My daddy gathered the rescue workers around Amanda and asked them to pray with him. We watched and listened while the strongest man I know gave his daughter back to her Father.

Complete numbness. Shock. Intense pain.

I don't remember blaming God.

Even though Daddy told me not to, deep inside I blamed myself.

The rest of my memory is hazy. I moved like a zombie through the pain and all the people and the food that they brought.

I cried and I watched Mama cry. My whole body ached under the weight of the deepest sorrow I had ever known in my life.

That day my world caved in and the mountains of my heart slid into the sea. I didn't know how to pray. Where was God? Was He mad at me? My sister had drowned in our backyard and maybe, just maybe, it was my fault. Amanda was gone, and the innocent hope that life would always be okay was taken with her.

Two years later, life came brutally rushing in again. This time it was December, and I was working on my chemistry homework in the kitchen. The phone rang, and a few minutes later, Mama screamed and fell back toward the wall. Aunt Bonnie had been taking flying lessons. She and her instructor were killed during a routine landing at the local airport. Their little plane had been caught in the wave of air that a jet creates when it takes off. The tower had given them permission to land too soon, and the strong wind that came from the jet smashed the nose of their plane down onto the runway.

Aunt Bonnie was thirty-eight when she died. She and Uncle Donald had two children, Donald Jr. and Cindy, my best friend, who was almost sixteen. We had lived in houses with adjoining backyards. We always went to the beach together. It was almost like we were just one big family.

I remember that my soul instinctively cried out for God. But again, this teenager who went to every church activity didn't know where God was or how to get to Him. I believed in the existence of God, but I didn't know what to believe about Him. Someone else I loved had been taken away in an instant. My best friend had lost her mother. Could anything be worse? What was God doing? How could I trust Him with my fragile hope?

In those young days, I was learning that life can sneak up on you at any time and punch you so hard that you think you'll never breathe again. Doubled over from the wallop that life had delivered, the earth moved again,

Life can sneak up on you at any time.

114

and the mountains that had been rebuilding in my heart slid back into the sea.

In a few more years, my grandfather went to heaven in his sleep after years of sickness. I was standing beside my grandmother at yet another funeral home when a man came by to offer his sympathies: "Ima, I'm sorry that your family has suffered and had to endure this trouble."

Without hesitation, my grandmother graciously replied, "Oh, honey, this is not trouble. Trouble is something you bring on yourself. This is just life."

My heart held on to those words, and they seemed to unlock some truth for me. I had believed that our family was plagued by trouble, but *what if this really was just life?* What if tragic loss, sickness, deep disappointment, and grieving hearts come to all those assigned to this earth? What if living means that suffering cannot be avoided?

I didn't understand the God I believed in. I didn't have a grasp on theology. But in those moments, I had a sense that maybe I had not caused these life tragedies. I felt guilty because I had not taken better care of Amanda. I felt guilty because I still had a mother when Cindy did not. If all of this was a part of living instead of punishment for crimes I couldn't see, maybe there could be freedom from the guilt. And maybe there was a reason to hope. God was calling me to Himself in those days, and my soul began to thirst for His truth.

Coming to Know Him

Since those years, I have come to know the God I could not find. I have met the One who heard me when I couldn't pray. The spiritual journey that began with a dry and thirsty soul led me to my sovereign Lord. I began to meet other people who really knew this God. I began to read the letters

He had written to me. I began to pray and ask for eyes that could see His work and ears that could hear His leading.

I now call this God Almighty, Savior, Provider, and Keeper, and I call myself His disciple. He is my Beloved, and I am His. I want to be like Jesus, aspiring to imitate His heart in mine. I have been pursuing God for many years and have been trained in the study of Scriptures and theology. I want my life to be built on the foundation of God's truth. I write about the reality of God's presence and the gift of salvation because of grace.

> The Lord is close to the brokenhearted and saves those who are crushed in spirit.
>
> Psalm 34:18

I talk to women about their spiritual lives and pray with my friends for God's leading, provision, and miracles. I have decided to stake my whole life on the truth that God is who He says He is and that Jesus Christ is His Son.

I am dancing with God, yet life just keeps coming. I imagine that I am not very different from you. Even though the details aren't the same, I expect that life just keeps coming for you too.

As a teenager, the earth shook underneath my feet, and my soul instinctively cried out for its Maker. But I knew Him only in theory from words I had heard or pictures in a book. I did not know the Creator in my heart.

Today, I am a follower of Christ, and when the earth begins to tremble and the mountains of my heart crumble toward the sea, my soul does what it was made to do—it cries out for the One who gives comfort and rest. The pain is still intense. The surprise attacks still take my breath away. But there is a difference now. The difference is that now I know the One who made my soul. Because of our dance together, because of His amazing provision and faithfulness to me, He is more than words in a book. He is my Father. He is my Provider. He is Mercy, and He is Hope.

Rain and Hurricanes

Jesus says that the rain falls on both the righteous and the unrighteous (Matthew 5:45), and none of us are exempt. An argument with your brother. A bad grade on a test. A friend moves out of state. And a little rain falls.

Seasons of brokenness can be very frustrating. The pain of loss in my teenage years was excruciating. But more than a little rain has fallen lately. In fact, even as I am writing, it feels like I'm standing on the shore while everyone else has evacuated and a hurricane is blowing through. I have been walking through one of the most difficult seasons of my life. I have felt harsh winds many times, but it has been a long time since the earth shook underneath me and I watched the mountains of my heart slide into the sea.

> Parts of our lives are no laughing matter. Hurricanes, especially, can be serious and devastating. Let's make it a point to laugh more. Find someone who makes you laugh and stand around that person today.

What began as a pattern of disappointment and grief has become the hurricane of a broken relationship. I am not wired for conflict. As a matter of fact, conflict makes me sleepy. It's my best coping technique. I usually retreat and wait until the coast is clear. But this time I have not been able to hide. I am standing in the middle of the most intense season of my life. There have been moments in these months when I could not seem to find my breath. There is a knot in my stomach from the pain. My head and my heart ache with great sadness. My eye is twitching. My

I am in pain, but I am being held in His great arms of comfort and protection.

hair is falling out. The stress has settled on me like a thick river fog. I have been ambushed by life, punched in the gut, and I'm struggling to withstand the relentless wind and rain.

The insulated life is not modeled for us in the life of Christ. Neither did the apostles find themselves sheltered from the storms of trials and persecution. We are a fallen people, walking through a fallen world, where all are tempted by the deceiver and many succumb to his snare. I should not be surprised that a blinding storm has blown into my life, but somehow I am.

Tender Mercy

A few weeks ago I was on the phone with a friend. I told her that my stomach felt sick over the disappointment and unknowing that I faced. She said, "Angela, you can't feel like that. You are the one who teaches about God's tender mercy. You have to model His strength in this." She meant well. I know her heart. But she missed it. Mercy is not the ability to no longer feel the pain and heartache of living in this world. Mercy is knowing that I am being held through the pain by my Father.

If a child is wounded, a mother doesn't say, "Brave soldier, do not feel the pain. Be strong like me." No way. A mother knows her children's cries. She runs to her child while he is still on the ground, picks him up, and carries him into the house. She checks the wound, applies compresses and bandages. She soothes him until the little warrior has been stilled in his heart. She waits until he's ready to wiggle away, strength renewed for the next backyard battle.

My heavenly Father is doing the same for me even now. I am in pain, but I am being held in His great arms of

Would you journal as much as you can about the storms that have come into your own life? Think about the surprise of their arrival . . . your heart during and after that season . . . your response to God and others . . . any lessons that you have learned.

comfort and protection. He is bandaging my wounds and quieting my soul with His gentle songs of love and affection. Right here, being held by my Savior, is God's tender mercy for my soul.

> Do you have wounds from the past that have never found healing? Show your battle scars now and ask for God's healing.
>
> _____
>
> _____
>
> _____
>
> _____
>
> _____

When the Father Holds You in His Arms

Sometimes the world tries to cut in, and we turn toward the distraction. Sometimes we hear the music of another land or choose the trappings of a lesser love. Sometimes we don't believe that the Lord of the dance is truly in love with us or that He sees us and desires a lifetime of love with us. And then sometimes it feels as though we're trying to dance, but the walls cave in and the floor gives way and we aren't really sure what just happened. Winds are blowing and a storm is raging and you can hear things like:

I'm so sorry, but your brother has leukemia.
You failed your exam.
We're filing for divorce.
I think I'm pregnant.

What I can promise you is that when hurricane winds

blow, the Father holds you close. You are tethered by His great love and devotion. In one of the darkest places I have ever known, the Lord is holding on to me in amazing and gracious ways.

A few days ago, after months of intense struggle, my emotions were so completely frayed that every tear in my body had to find its way to the surface and spill. I am not sure that I have ever cried so hard or so loud or so long. I could not carry one more piece of information or pretend to be strong one more minute. It all had to be laid down. The process of handing over my broken heart left me lying on the floor like a rag doll.

My dear friend called me at the end of this day and, from half a country away, held me with the power of God. She cried with me and prayed gentle prayers. And before we said goodbye, she said, "Angela, I want you to let God calm your soul by focusing on His call to be still. In whatever comes to you next, say, 'Be still,' so that you can know the presence of God."

The gentle reminder from my friend to pray words from the Bible was the Father's healing salve for my pain. My body was weary, and I thought that I could not move, but God's stillness let me stand and move through the evening until the stillness of night brought His peace.

The next day, God sent a friend to hold me in the comfort of her hug and speak into my heart. "You are stronger than you know. God has not abandoned you. I promise that this season will pass. I will walk with you every step of the way. I will hold you before the Lord in fervent prayer."

Yesterday was a day of distraction. A drive through the mountains. The windows down, a few wrong turns, beautiful views, and laughter. My head needed a few moments to forget so that my heart could begin to recover.

One of my favorite passages in all of Scripture is Psalm 46:1–3:

> God is our refuge and strength, an ever-present help in trouble.
>
> Therefore we will not fear, though the earth give way and the mountains fall into the heart of the sea,
>
> Though its waters roar and foam and the mountains quake with their surging.

Who could use a positive word from you today? Ask God to send you to help a friend in need—then do it!

God is using these words over and over in my heart. He is teaching me again that I do not have to be afraid in this dark place. I cannot see one sign that reveals how God is going to work. I do not have any power to manipulate or favors to call in. My hands are tied, and my struggles will certainly multiply unless God shows up and intervenes. I am desperate. Even though my world seems to have caved in and the floor has given way, I am assured by this passage that the strong arms of Mercy are holding me.

Has the earth been rumbling underneath your feet? Did life sneak up on you and punch you so hard that you've lost your breath? Are you walking in a dark place, unable to see, fumbling for any door to get out? Are you afraid of your circumstances? Your accusers? The rumors? Do you fear that the winds of life will surely blow you away? Then hear these words of assurance and refuge: *the only hope we have is the only hope we've ever had.*

My Deliverer

Our only hope is our best hope, and He is the Lord God Almighty. Invincible Warrior. Fearless Protector. Merciful Father.

We are held and guarded by the same God who led the Israelites from bondage under hot pursuit by Pharaoh and his troops. This is our wild and relentless God who will fight for those who belong to Him. This is the God who fears nothing, not the Egyptians, not Pharaoh, and certainly not the hurricanes that blow through our lives.

Do you remember that before God parted the sea, the Israelites were scared spitless? The Egyptians were closing in. The sea was before them. There was nowhere to go and no way out. Imminent death was certain, and they cried out in their faithlessness, "Where is this God who is going to save us? He has surely brought us here to die."

Going back even seemed better than having no hope. They wanted to return to Pharaoh's bondage and live in the shackles of slavery—anything but stand before a sea of raging hopelessness with the enemy breathing down their necks.

Now, these are the people who had just watched God deliver ten plagues to the Egyptians to get His point across. These are the same ones who have been freed from slavery and not just meekly released, mind you, with only the clothes on their backs. They left Egypt as conquerors with the flocks and herds of the Egyptians, plus all of their silver and gold. Exodus 12:36 says that because of the Lord's provision, the Israelites "plundered the Egyptians."

God kept vigil until all His people were delivered (Exodus 12:42) and then visibly led them step after step in a pillar of cloud by day and a pillar of fire by night to light the way (Exodus 13:21). God didn't just deliver His people. He showed up in glory and brilliance to fight for the ones He loved.

Be Still and Watch

I must confess to you that I can look more like a faithless Israelite than the image we have conjured up of godly women. I have watched God's hand in my life, and I have journals that record His constant provision and protection. God has always taken care of me. I know that more than I know anything. Yet, in my humanness, in my weakness, and in my sinfulness, I too can stand at the sea, with the earth quaking beneath me, with fury at my back, and cry out to God, "Where are You? What are You doing? I don't think I can do this. Let me go back. Anything—just not this."

And then Moses says to the Israelites (and to me) in Exodus 14:13–14:

> Do not be afraid. Stand firm and you will see the deliverance the LORD will bring to you today. The Egyptians you see today you will never see again. The LORD will fight for you; you need only to be still.

In effect, Moses was saying to God's people, "The only hope you have is the only hope you've ever had. There is no other way. Now stand still and watch Him fight."

Our God will not be dissuaded from His purpose. Our lack of faith does not undo His love for us. Our weaknesses are not His. He stands ready. He never looks away. He is always and eternally in charge.

Do you hear what God is saying to us? Do not be afraid of the circumstances that cause you pain and choke the breath from you. Do not fear the ones who want to over-take you or the sea that blocks your way. Do not look back or run and hide. Stand still, and watch God show up in all His glory.

And that, dear one, is our call. It was my friend's wis-dom, the command of Moses, and the words of God writ-ten in the Psalms: "Be still and know that I am God" (46:10).

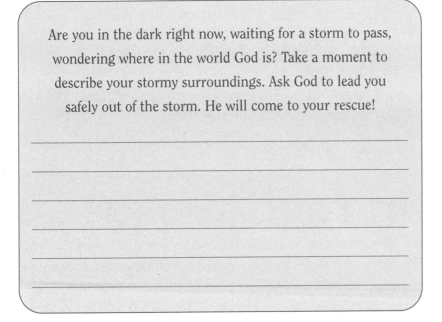

Are you in the dark right now, waiting for a storm to pass, wondering where in the world God is? Take a moment to describe your stormy surroundings. Ask God to lead you safely out of the storm. He will come to your rescue!

_____

_____

_____

_____

_____

_____

When your world caves in. When the lights go out. When devastating news arrives. When fools rush in. When you have done everything you can and find yourself crushed by the weight of doing—right there is where God wants you to stop and be stilled. Stand before the only hope you have . . . and wait.

Standing in the dark without hope can be catastrophic. We have only to witness the depression that surrounds us, the addictions that consume lives, and the growing rate of suicide the world over. People who stand in the dark without hope will self-destruct. But hope comes in the stillness. In the still places, God whispers, "Do you know who I am? Nothing is too hard for Me. I love doing this stuff. I love fighting for My beloved. Now stop wringing your hands and watch Me."

God shows us that His glory is always worth the wait. Remember the end of this story?

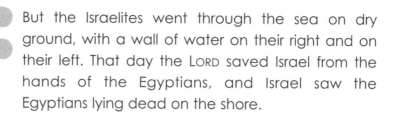

But the Israelites went through the sea on dry ground, with a wall of water on their right and on their left. That day the LORD saved Israel from the hands of the Egyptians, and Israel saw the Egyptians lying dead on the shore.

Exodus 14:29–30

Amazing.

A whole nation walks through a sea on dry land. A whole army is drowned in the water behind them. Do you think that there was one person standing on the shore thinking, *If God would just part this water, then we could cross over and be saved from the Egyptians?* No way. There was no one who could have imagined what the Lord would do. But God did one of His best God-things. Our Deliverer did what He has promised to do for you and me. He showed up when all the options had expired so that He could get the glory.

What was God trying to do anyway? Why did He wait until the last minute? Why didn't He write His plan on a tablet and pass it around so that everyone could feel better? The next verse gives us some insight:

His glory is always worth the wait.

And when the Israelites saw the great power the LORD displayed against the Egyptians, the people feared the LORD and *put their trust in him* . . .

Exodus 14:31 (emphasis mine)

Does God want us to trust Him? You bet He does. Do you give your trust out indiscriminately? Not me. I'm hesitant. I want evidence that someone is trustworthy. God knew that if His people could see His magnificent power, they would deem Him worthy of their trust—a trust they would need for generations to come.

Do you trust God? I mean really? I wrestle with it almost moment by moment these days. My theology says that I trust God. I hear my mouth say that I trust God. I pray and tell God that I trust Him. But more than anything I want to live in the power of that truth. I will believe that I am strong one day only to feel my trust bending under the strain of gusting winds the next.

God knows that life can throw us up against a wall with no options and that the pain can be intense. But He stands vigil over us like a pillar of cloud and fire. We are beautiful to Him, and His eye is continually upon us. He will be our strength and refuge while we wait in the dark. He will hold us as a Father holds His wounded child. He delights to fight our battles. He wants to rescue us from the encroaching rings of fire. He wants to do what we cannot even imagine.

He wants us to know that He is the only hope we'll ever have.

If there is a question attached to a girl's soul, maybe it's "Do you think I'm beautiful?" When God answers from the depth of His great love, it makes some of us feel like the wallflower who is asked to dance. But we can become distracted from His invitation because of the other loves, whispers of unbelief, noise and clutter, and because we are sometimes the prodigal, sometimes the elder brother. To return to the music and strong embrace of God requires a desperate and pursuing heart. And when a girl chooses to remain in His arms of devotion, God gives the only hope we have

and His perfect love.

Chapter 9

His Perfect Love

There is a story about a man who works at a bungee jump. Atop several stories, he stands on a platform, paid to carefully strap in those who want to step over into nothing, scream with fear, lose their breath, bounce upside down, and dangle. He wears a T-shirt that reads, "Shut Up and Jump!"

I told my friend Dennis that story and then added, "I need a T-shirt like his. In my life right now, I am standing on a platform scared to death, afraid to jump, and ready to chat. I'm all talk and no jump. As a matter of fact, I would rather talk about anything than jump . . . fifty ways to jump, fifty ways not to jump, velocity, wind speed, appropriate jumping attire, other people who've jumped before me—anything to avoid my fears."

We laughed together, and then Dennis said, "Tell me why you're so afraid."

"I don't know exactly. Maybe I'm afraid that I'm not tied on."

"Tied on how?"

"Tied on to God."

There was a patient sigh, and then Dennis said, "Angela, you are more tied on than you know. Well, maybe you know it up in that head of yours, but you have forgotten with your heart."

"Dennis, what if I make a mistake?"

"Don't you understand? Even if you make a mistake, God still has you. You are tied on with a bond that cannot be broken. And when you are tied on to God, Angela, you do not have to be afraid."

> Do you wonder if you are truly tied on to God?
> What makes you wonder?
>
> _____
>
> _____
>
> _____
>
> _____
>
> _____

Jumping

I have never jumped from a bungee platform or parachuted from a plane. But I have walked with God and imagine that sometimes it can feel about the same. There has to be a time between jumping and being "caught" when you are scared to death, praying your guts out, and hoping against hope that something is going to grab you and save your life.

Sometimes life requires us to jump into the realm of the unknown.

Sometimes life leaves us waiting in the dark.

Sometimes life throws us from the train and yells, "Find your own way home!"

The moments between jumping and being caught, the days that keep you sitting in the dark and waiting alone, the season of staggering that comes from being tossed aside—each can be a holy place . . . a holy place called trust.

I will be honest with you: when life pulls one of those loop de loops just as I think I'm coasting, my knee-jerk reaction is not always trust. More often than not I succumb instantly to fear . . . afraid of falling . . . afraid of the dark . . . afraid of being lost and never finding my way home. Afraid of almost anything, actually.

How many girls does that happen to? How many of us love God and still let His enemy called Fear into our homes? Not only do we open the door and ask him in, we invite him to stay for dinner and then later we let him crawl right into bed with us. And so there we are, tucked underneath our cozy blankets with Fear snuggled up beside us.

Most of the women I know are beset with fear. It looms in the shadows where others can't see and bullies us with unrelenting intimidation. Fear kicks us under the table, elbows us in the ribs, and pinches us when no one is looking. Fear tells us that we deserve punishment and then keeps us in a head-lock until we scream, "Okay, okay, I believe it!"

If you knew God was calling you to free-fall headfirst into an adventure, the one He has planned for you, would you do it?

131

Fear yells, "You can't," to make us stop.

Fear cries, "You could get hurt," to send us packing.

Fear asks, "What if they knew all your sin?" to steal our forgiveness.

Fear snickers, "You don't deserve anything," to dismantle our dreams.

Fear plays with your head, rips out your heart, and empties the soul of strength and determination and will.

I have done battle with the bully Fear. I begin to think of myself as a conqueror, and then a gang of new Fears will appear, seemingly to avenge the battles I've already won.

Right now, right at this moment, I am afraid to write. Great timing, huh? Why couldn't I be afraid to write when I don't have a deadline? I know that I have been called to this message. I am truly excited about it and feel like I have a few stories to tell and some Scripture to unfold that will help us pursue the heart of God. It would take an entire afternoon to tell you how God has orchestrated this process. At every turn, He has affirmed that I am supposed to do this work. So why in the world am I afraid?

Maybe I'm afraid that I won't be enough.

Maybe I compare myself to an endless list of writers in my head.

Maybe I'm worried that I'll miss God's leading.

Do you recognize the whispers of unbelief that speak into my heart and paralyze my soul with fear? Does unbelief ever whisper into your ear and make you afraid?

I want to jump into the arms of God and free-fall headfirst into His adventure. But Fear has climbed the stairs with me and is trying to talk me out of it. God is yelling, "Fall into My arms. You are tied on. I have you. Come on, Angela, jump to Me." And Fear is questioning, "Are you sure? What

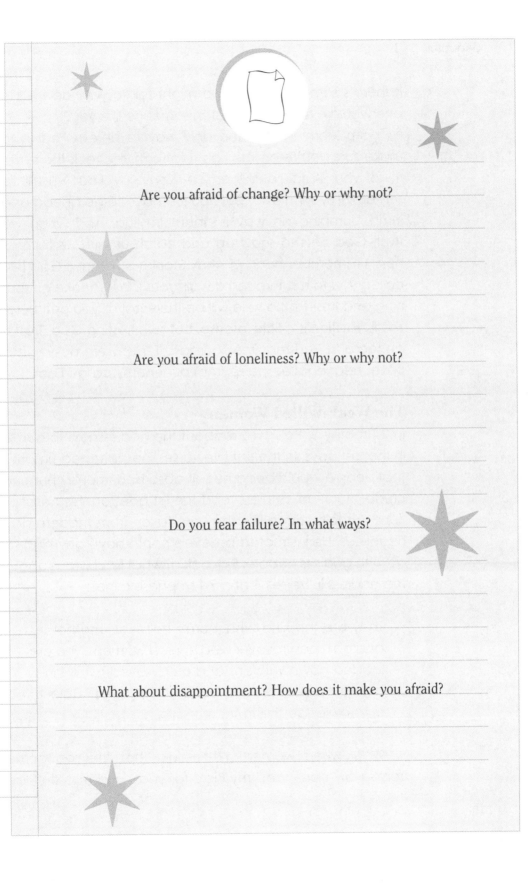

Are you afraid of change? Why or why not?

Are you afraid of loneliness? Why or why not?

Do you fear failure? In what ways?

What about disappointment? How does it make you afraid?

if there's some mistake? You might fall to your death. No one would ever want to catch someone like you."

I am learning that the only way to defeat Fear is to make sure you're on the right platform, recheck the security of your straps, and then *jump anyway*. Fear will still be screaming your name, but you just have to go ahead and jump. Jumping anyway is about trusting. And when we trust, God gets to show up and catch us with His faithfulness. I remember hearing Andy Stanley say that if God has called you to run through a wall, your job is to take off running and trust that a hole will be there just as you get there. The illustration is a little intense, but so is trusting God. Trust is dangerous. Trust requires courage. If trust were easy, we'd never hear another peep from our enemy called Fear.

The Weak-Willed Woman

In 2 Timothy 3, Paul wrote about the godlessness to come in the last days. In the first five verses, he instructed Timothy that people would become self-absorbed, money-hungry, crude, stuck-up, ruthless, and the list goes on. His descriptions actually sound like they are taken from modern-day headlines. He instructed believers not to have anything to do with godless people. But look at what Paul wrote about the godless in verses 6 and 7 (emphasis mine):

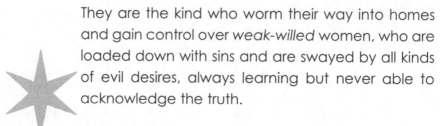

> They are the kind who worm their way into homes and gain control over *weak-willed* women, who are loaded down with sins and are swayed by all kinds of evil desires, always learning but never able to acknowledge the truth.

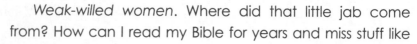

Weak-willed women. Where did that little jab come from? How can I read my Bible for years and miss stuff like that? I probably always thought Paul was talking about someone else, women back in Bible days, but not me. I could never be a weak-willed woman. In *The Message*, Eugene Peterson calls them "unstable and needy women." I don't know about you, but I don't really like the implication here. It makes me cringe to think that I could have "weak-willed" potential. Actually, it kind of makes me mad. But I must set aside the temptation to be insulted and examine my own heart for truth. Have I ever been weak-willed? Yes. Do I want to live like that? Absolutely not.

So, what do you think Paul meant by a weak-willed woman? I'll see if I can describe it, but—careful—it may hit too close to home. I believe that a weak-willed woman is consumed with her fears. As a matter of fact, it's fear that makes her unstable and needy. She is self-absorbed and cares more than she can admit about what everyone else thinks of her. She may have been beaten down and stayed there, or she may be loud, brash, and dominant but weak-willed. She has lost her ambition and passion, but she desires to control the lives of others. She isn't really sure that God loves her just as she is, and she's never even considered that He calls her beautiful. Her starving soul tries to get its filling from others, and when they don't give enough, she retreats into self-pity and then depression.

She can harbor a grudge, play around with gossip, and discreetly indulge her obsessions with the best of them. She is easily hurt or offended. She is spiritually knowledgeable but essentially lost. She goes to Bible studies, but her life never really changes because

A weak-willed woman
is easy prey.

there is nothing inside her for the truth to latch on to—her will to become and grow is weak. Did I mention that she has a critical spirit? She does, and it's painful to watch her get wound up.

Should I go on, or do you get the picture? A weak-willed woman is easy prey for the attacks of an enemy. She is defenseless and easily controlled by the godlessness that can worm its way into her home. When evil breaks down the door and finds this cowering woman, her weakness becomes frailty, her instability becomes emotional distress, and the spiritual spiral is downward.

Can you see the cause of this whole mess? What keeps a weak-willed woman weak? What drains the very life out of her and leaves her floundering? What makes her spirit bitter and empties her soul? It's fear . . . the unyielding bully that hides in the shadows.

What are we all so afraid of? I spoke to this a bit earlier, but let's wade in a little deeper.

We fear change. Forget that change could mean receiving God's best. We still cling to our old familiar thoughts, ideas, and ways of coping. No change, please. It's disconcerting. We like things just the way they are and then wonder why we've grown bored.

Someone once said that the only thing you can be sure of is that everything will change. Every time I get my books put into freshly painted shelves, alphabetized by author, and sectioned by content, it's time to pack them up and move them to another set of shelves miles away. I am getting to know my books pretty well by now and am learning to give away a few boxes with every move. Right this minute, some are on makeshift shelving, and some are still packed away. I am anticipating that I have not seen the last of my book boxes and, for some reason, I'm okay with that. I think I have confronted the bully of change enough that he doesn't scare me so much anymore. He used to eat my lunch every time.

If we learn to welcome change that is coming anyway, we can move out of the shadows of great fear and into the light of expectancy.

We also fear heartache, pain, and suffering. Women can be given to great depths of heartache. We have been made to feel deeply and be moved by emotion. So much good comes from our touchy-feely selves. Tender memories are made. Hearts and bodies are cared for. Homes are brightened and blessed. But this gift of feeling can also leave a girl torn and racked with pain. Misunderstandings. Lost love. Intense grief. Intentional wounds. For every relationship in a woman's life, there is an opportunity for heartache. We've had enough pain already, and so we retreat. We pull back. We decline graciously. We decide to live quietly, skip the adventure, and stay away from the spotlight. That way, maybe the bully of heartache won't find us.

If we could somehow understand that there are no suffering exemptions for the living, maybe we would not give our minds over to such depths of worry and fear. Heartache is the by-product of a fallen world, broken relationships, and Satan's work. We will not avoid it. There is no such thing as an insulated life. Even the girl who you think has it all together and seems to have every material blessing walks the same path you do—one full of twists and turns of heartache where she can be ambushed by the bully of suffering.

Tell Him about your fears.

We fear loneliness. I think that I like to be alone, and I do—for about six hours. Then I've had enough. I want everyone to come back home, the phone to start ringing, and something fun to begin gearing up. Solitude can quickly give way to loneliness, especially for girls, it seems. Even worse is when you find yourself in the middle of a busy schedule, yet find loneliness haunting you from the shadows.

We have been made for relationships, and this fear says that one day we'll turn around and there will be no one. No one who knows us. No one who can make us laugh. No one to cry with. No one to hold us. I am tempted to remind you that Jesus said He would always be with us. I actually take great comfort in His words. But I can hear a few of you saying, "Thank you for the nice Bible verse, but I am still plagued with loneliness, and I fear that it will get worse." I hear you. I understand the yearning. For hugs. Audible words. Dinner and dancing. There are some elements of relationship that I won't have with Jesus until I step into His presence in heaven. But He can still provide.

Tell Him about your fears and ask Him to fight this one for you. Entrust Him with your heart. Be honest about the depth of your desire. But don't hide. Hiding feeds the fear of loneliness. Step out into the light and watch Him come to provide. He delivers kisses and hugs in the most delightful ways. He directs angels to make phone calls and write notes. And He can even surprise you with a Friday night movie date. Just you wait. Wait right there in His presence and see how He comes to provide.

We fear failure. What if I step onto the stage of adventure and trip over my shoelaces? What if the audience boos or the curtain falls on my head? What if the director yells, "Cut. Next, please"? What if the cast members snicker?

What if the play is a flop? What if I get bad reviews? What if . . . what if . . . what if? To fear failure is to live under the heaviness of what-ifs . . . to remain in the dressing room when you've been called center-stage . . . to settle for your antics in the bathroom mirror when you know you've been made for the theater.

When I was a sophomore in college I did very poorly in an advanced accounting class. I was aching over the bad grades and feeling like I was doomed to failure in the business world. A friend from the same class called me one night and said, "You know, Angela, your grade in that class is not an indicator of how successful you will be in life." I decided to believe him, and the principle continues to impact my thinking. Failure is not dying. Failure is not the end unless it keeps you from trying again. Maybe instead of failure, we'd do better to fear the death of dreaming.

We fear disappointment. The biggest enemy of hope is the fear of disappointment. It tethers our celebration. It tempers our praise. We hold on and hold back, afraid to get too excited about anything. Sometimes I think, *Doggone it, I know what disappointment feels like. I know the pain of being let down. I know the agony of dashed desire, the sorrow of treasures lost, and the humiliation of a reputation tarnished. I know what it feels like to be thoroughly baffled by circumstances. I know what disappointment feels like, but I don't know so much about the great joy of hope. It's time for me to risk it so that I can know. And so, I'm choosing . . . wild hope, reckless expectancy, mountaintop singing, and happy dancing.*

Call me crazy, but I'm tired of being held back by the fear of disappointment. I am learning to say, "Move over, handwringers. Stand back, all you naysayers. One party of hope coming through!"

We fear rejection. It's happened to all of us. Dumped. Overlooked. Sent packing. Oh, the great and devastating pain of rejection. Country music songwriters would have little to write about apart from the severe suffering that comes from unrequited love and refusal. And their music wouldn't be so popular if the ache weren't universal.

Whether you got passed over for the part in the play, you were the only one not invited to the sleepover, or some guy told you it was over, there is a misery attached to being left out, forgotten, or turned away. The bully whispers, "See, I've been trying to tell you that no one has ever wanted you. You have nothing to contribute. Just give up and go to the back of the line." His words are painful, but we believe them. We step back, isolate, and become hesitant. We reserve our love and padlock our hearts. We sit in the shadows and cry for the freedom of acceptance.

In order to become or do anything with our lives, we have to walk past the fear of rejection. He will play chicken with us and dare us to cross the line he's drawn in our dreams. He will jeer and taunt us with every baby step of courage we take. He might even chase us around the corner, but he is only a bully, and bullies always lose when you stop believing them.

The weak-willed woman is mocked by the bully of fear. She recoils and he loves it. She cries out in pain and he gets in her face. The bully pushes and ridicules until he provokes her to anger, then he twists her words and throws them back at her as spears of doubt and confusion. She finally breaks into a million pieces, and he leans back to laugh at her tears.

But the weak-willed woman has a friend who comes to her rescue. He steps into the back alley of pain and stands head and shoulders above fear. He appears in the nick of time to free the woman from the grip of terror. Just the sight of this friend makes the bully run away. The friend is courageous and strong. He is undaunted and valiant. He is a hero and a conqueror. The friend who rescues the weak-willed woman is the one called Perfect Love.

In the Same Room As Love

Perfect love is from God, and His perfect love casts out all the bullies of fear.

I hope the Lord won't mind, and you won't mind, if I very loosely paraphrase this passage according to the themes we've been discussing.

God is love.

The woman who dances in the arms of God has God's love in her.

God's love fills up the whole room so that there are no shadows where bullies can hide.

God's love gives a woman righteous confidence.

Read what John had to say about perfect love:

God is love.
Whoever lives in love lives in God, and God in him.
In this way, love is made complete among us so that we will have confidence on the day of judgment, because in this world we are like him.
There is no fear in love.
But perfect love drives out fear, because fear has to do with punishment.
The one who fears is not made perfect in love.
1 John 4:16–18

Now, underline the words that speak directly to you.

He loves her like He loves Christ, and that should take away all her worries about Judgment Day.

There is no place for fear in the same room as love.

Perfect Love chases away the bullies of fear because all they want to do is make you believe that you deserve punishment.

The woman who fears is not dancing in the arms of Perfect Love.

When you and I are in the arms of God, we are being held by His perfect love. John wrote that perfect love drives out fear. To be free of the fear that grips our souls is to remain desperate for the intimacy of God. When we are in the same room as that great love, we are walking in the light of His mercy and grace and freedom. In the light, there are no shadows. Without shadows, there is no place for fear to hide. Fear cannot stalk you from the light.

I have been afraid for so long, but I do not want to be afraid anymore. Some of my greatest spiritual battles have been in regard to overcoming fear. These battles are intense, and they can scorch the soul. Their cinders reignite long after I think the fire has been put out. I can once again listen to the bully I thought I'd forgotten. When I feel the bully yank my hair or hear him heckle me from the front row, I am learning to run with everything I have into the presence of God.

I fall on my face and lie on my floor and pray desperate prayers: *God, rescue me from the bully. God, come quickly; I do not want to be taunted today. God, send ten thousand angels to cover me with their protection. God, let*

I do not want to be afraid anymore.

me believe Your truth instead of the lies. Stand me up in strength with renewed courage and power. Go before me. Hold me. Defend me.

The power of a bully is neutralized when you quit believing him. I don't want to spend any more days in the grip of his deceit and confusion.

Sometimes running into the presence of God means calling someone safe and telling them that fear has crept in. Someone who will understand. A person of grace. Someone who will pray. My friend Dennis will e-mail me, "I've got your back this week." That means he is in the battle with me. From thousands of miles away, he and his wife, Karen, are praying into my fears and asking God to keep me safe.

John says in that passage that the bully of fear wants you to believe you deserve punishment. The bully never relents. He keeps pounding you with your past. Over and over he reminds you of the mistakes. He makes up what-ifs. He recalls the hurt and rips open old wounds.

Indulge me a brief theology lesson on position. We would deserve punishment except for Jesus. Jesus has already paid for everything. *Everything.* God said that

> What kind of girl might you be without your fears? Go ahead and envision yourself a fearless woman. You would be amazing! What would you do? Where would you go? Who would you reach out to?
>
> _____
> _____
> _____
> _____
> _____
> _____
> _____
> _____
> _____
>
> Sooo, what's stopping ya?!

Jesus' death on the cross was enough . . . enough to pay for the punishment we deserve. He says that when we claim Jesus' payment for our sins, our position is the same as His Son. We become sons and daughters of God. We become just like Jesus in the eyes of God. We have the same position as Christ.

It's a little mind-boggling because we can't comprehend such forgiveness. We cannot wrap our minds around such grace. But the truth of your position is that you do not deserve punishment anymore. You must unlearn everything you have believed. Where there is perfect love, there cannot be fear because fear has to do with believing that you still deserve punishment. The bully and his lies cannot be in the same room with God. His perfect love for you will drive them out.

Fear is the enemy of everything God wants to bring forth from your life. Fear will stop a woman dead in her tracks and keep her there for years—even decades. Fear will keep you from your God-given dreams and ambition. Fear will make you deny your gifts and turn a deaf ear to your calling. If you are going to move forward, if you are going to participate in the life God imagined when He thought of you, if you are going to drink deeply from the well of passion and grace, you must run with everything you have into the strong arms of God and let His perfect love drive out every fear.

I have climbed the platform of my ambition. The flight of steps leads toward my dreams and aspirations. I know for sure this is the place God has called me to. Every path has led in this direction. Every counsel has affirmed His plan. Friends have climbed steps with me. Others have prayed me up from down below.

Finally, I am at the top, and I can see the unfolding

view of God's design. This is not the end but the first of many platforms to come. It has taken so long to climb this one, and I get to the top with aching muscles, a little out of breath. But Fear has climbed with me. He is laughing at my aches and pains. He says that I should be in better shape if I'm going to get to the next platform. He makes me feel worthless. He leans into my weakness and pushes every button.

I stand at the top of my calling, listening to the doubts that surround me. I decide to talk it through. Ask a few more people. Weigh each fear and discuss the implications. Maybe I should do more research. Maybe I don't deserve this now. Maybe I should go back down the steps and rethink the whole thing. Fear has raised some good issues.

But a gentle voice calls to me. It is the most confident voice I have ever heard. He is not impatient. He is not flustered. It sounds like He is speaking to me through a smile. He is calm and assured. He is strong and persuasive.

Perfect Love yells to me, "Angela, you are tied on. I promise. This is the place I have led you to. This is exactly the right time. You are not a weak-willed woman anymore because you are desperate for Me. Tell Fear to step aside. Trust Me. I have you. **NOW, SHUT UP AND JUMP!**"

If there is a question attached to a girl's soul, maybe it's "Do you think I'm beautiful?" When God answers from the depth of His great love, it makes some of us feel like the wallflower who is asked to dance. But we can become distracted from His invitation because of the other loves, whispers of unbelief, noise and clutter, and because we are sometimes the prodigal, sometimes the elder brother. To return to the music and strong embrace of God requires a desperate and pursuing heart. And when a girl chooses to remain in His arms of devotion, God gives the only hope we have: His perfect love

and a beautiful crown.

Chapter 10

A Beautiful Crown

About every other weekend I get on an airplane bound for somewhere I've never been so that I can get into a car with someone I've never met. At the destination, I'm usually looking for a smiling woman who acts like she knows me or has a card with my name on it.

Except there was the time when I was the last person waiting at baggage claim. A somber-looking woman had been standing across the room watching me ever since I walked through the gate. After I retrieved my bags, I walked over to ask if she might be my ride. She opened up a folded card with my name on it, and I said, "Yep, that's me. It's nice to meet you."

She seemed a bit hesitant and flustered, but finally stammered out, "Well, it's just that you don't look like anyone who's ever spoken at our church before."

I flashed her one of those my-confidence-is-shot-but-I'm-smiling-anyway smiles, gave her a big you're-gonna-like-me-if-it's-the-last-thing-you-do hug, and silently asked God to break down the barriers and connect us at the heart. He did because He always does, and I never quite

figured out what the problem was. Maybe the black go-go boots threw her. Oh, and I was the only girl in pants all weekend. But other than that I'm not really sure what she meant.

But usually I get into a car with a woman I've just met so that she can take me to a place I've never seen. By the time we arrive, it feels like we've known each other forever, and then she hands me off to the next person. Stranger number two becomes another fast friend. She shows me around, gives me an overview of the weekend, and then carts me off to dinner and later onto an unfamiliar bed to sleep.

It's another women's conference, and I love them! What's not to love? Highly creative and crafty women have worked for months planning themes, food, location, ambience, goodie bags, and more details than an over-booked wedding planner. They have prayed and searched for the heart of God in every decision. Add to all that a few hundred women who don't get out much, and you've got a full-blown party just waiting to happen.

For me, the party begins with a plane ride and strangers. It ends with a whole room full of new friends and hugs all around, but there is no telling what will happen in between.

Late one Friday, my plane was delayed, and I arrived at the conference center just as I was supposed to speak. I shook hands with the hostess, clipped on the cordless mike, and hurried up to the platform. Finally settled, I took my first look out at the women. Every single one of them was wearing the plastic shower cap that came in their gift bags. Someone threw one up to me, and for the first and only time in my life, God willing, I spoke as convincingly as I could in a shower cap.

Another time, I walked into a conference room for my first meeting with a group of women. Immediately a lady walked over to me and said, "I'd feel a whole lot better if you were about twenty years older and had gray hair."

I'm thinking, *I'd feel a whole lot better if you hadn't just said that*, but mumbled out something like, "Well, let's see if God shows up anyway."

About an hour later during the break, she came to me with tears streaming down her face. "I'm sorry about what I said," she whispered. "I am realizing that my soul has been fast asleep."

"Sounds like God's showing up."

"Yes, He's here."

I held her for a long time and silently thanked God for using somebody twenty years younger with five shades of blonde in her hair. What a privilege to watch Him move.

Over the years I've received all kinds of compliments that make me chuckle. Things like,

I thought you were just going to be some kind of fluff head.

You make me sick when you start with that perky stuff first thing in the morning.

What you said was so simple, I could have said it.

You know you shouldn't get carried away with that grace stuff; people might just get the wrong idea about you.

Has anyone ever told you that you look like Jan Brady from The Brady Bunch?

Sounds like God's showing up.

Has anyone ever told you that you look like Hillary Clinton?

I have a dog named Angela.

We've been sitting on the front row all weekend listening to you speak, and the one thing we have to know is, what kind of lipstick do you wear? It never smeared and stayed on the whole time.

Zingers like those make me laugh, but they also keep my heart in check and call me back to truth.

Weekends with the Girls

The weekends are not about me. Never have been and never will be. Nothing will happen in the heart or soul of a woman apart from the astounding presence of Jesus. I have been called to show up and stand up and beg God for His words in spite of me. Oh my goodness, He knows it's just me. Sinner me. Fallen me. Struggling me. And from His heart of grace, He continues to be faithful to use *me*. It is an honor to hang out with women and tell them about the depths of God's incomprehensible love. It is a relief to trust that everything good and powerful comes directly from God's hand into the heart of each woman.

One recent Sunday morning, the conference was winding down with our final time together. I did not have to speak because the hour was slated for sharing. Women could stand up if they wanted to and tell others what God was doing in their lives. We sang for a while and then sat quietly waiting to see if anyone wanted to speak.

There was an awkward silence before a brave woman

made her way up from the back. "I've been at this church for two years now." She spoke through tears. "Some of my deepest wounds have come from past relationships in the church, and so, since we came here, I have just been standing back waiting to see which one of you was going to hurt me. It hasn't happened. God is doing something different in my heart. I feel myself becoming softer. I want to be your friend. I am not as afraid as I used to be."

The next woman came up to say, "Some of you know that I am going through a divorce. It feels like my whole world has fallen apart. I expected you to paint a big *D* on my back and stay as far away from me as possible. I think I expected that God would do that to me too. He hasn't and you haven't. Thank you for still loving me."

Another woman stood and confessed an abortion in her past. She thanked God for her teenage children and the compassionate husband who forgave her.

Another wept openly because of the recent death of her child and told of the strength she was receiving for each day.

But the story that ripped my heart out belonged to the last woman. She was small and quiet. The entire weekend she had worked in the background and seemed to hide in the details of things to be done. When she got to the front, she could barely speak through her sobs. "All my life I have asked God why He made me short and unattractive. All my life I have wished I could be anybody else but me. This morning, a woman put her hands on my face and said, 'God thinks that you are beautiful.' I've never heard anything like that before. I can't tell you how it makes me feel to think that it might be true. God thinks I am beautiful."

There wasn't a woman in the room without a handful of wadded up tissues and mascara stains on her face.

The sharing that had begun with timidity ended up lasting a couple of hours. Over and over, women stood and spoke powerfully, personally, and with incredible transparency. It wasn't long until the theme became obvious. Abortion, insecurity, addiction, sexual abuse, emotional abuse, death, rejection, failure, divorce, and loss . . . very few women had been left unscathed by some kind of heartache or pain. But as each woman stood to tell her story, we heard about the God who replaces the ashes of broken lives with crowns of beauty.

Beauty for ashes. What a trade. Only a God who's wildly in love would do that.

> I just finished reading *Do You Think I'm Beautiful.* I have been on the verge of suicide, wanting to leave my church and my pain. The Lord used this message, among other things, to speak His love over me. I'm simply overwhelmed at how much He loves me. I'm still hurting, but I know that He's with me.
>
> —Grace

The Ash Heap

Ever sat in your ash heap and wondered how in the world God could do anything with your pile of cinders? Have you ever given up on yourself and expected that God must do the same? Have you woken up so tired and achy and burdened with pain that you'd rather not do another day? Have you let yourself believe that the wounds you've received and the mistakes you've made will surely ruin the rest of your life?

Some girls sit in the ashes of deep woundedness . . . the addictions of a parent, the distance of a father, the anger of a mom, abandonment, rape, incest, emotional or mental abuse. These girls grieve the pain of their memories, curse the ugliness of their scars, and cry for the lives that have been stolen from them.

If you could look into your sack of ashes, what would be in there?

_____

_____

_____

_____

_____

_____

Write or pray about the ashes inside of you that need to be poured out.

_____

_____

_____

_____

_____

_____

_____

_____

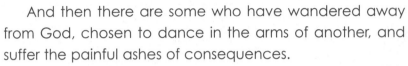

And then there are some who have wandered away from God, chosen to dance in the arms of another, and suffer the painful ashes of consequences.

Most of the women I know carry a sack full. Ashes they've acquired by choice or no choice or crummy ashes they've been forced to haul around. Sometimes we drag the sack along behind us and sometimes we dump the whole thing out and sit in them for a while or for a lifetime.

But if you are not one of those girls, you may be thinking, *Angela, I really don't have an ash heap. I can't point to anything in my life that has caused me great pain or severely wounded my soul. Actually, I'm not even sure I need this book. Life is really okay. I kind of think I'm beautiful. I know God is in love with me. My family loves me. I enjoy my life. There have been some disappointments, but nothing really major. I feel pretty strong and capable. Life is good, and mostly, it's great.*

If it sounds like I know what you're thinking, it's because I have been you. Most of my life has been happy and healthy. No particular bag of ashes to carry. No big scars to point to with pain or regret. I knew early that I wasn't really beautiful, but not "U-G-L-Y, you ain't got no alibi" kind of ugly, and besides, you learn to live with that stuff. There was laughter, a sense of purpose, friends, and an incredible family. I knew that God loved me and every decision and new path always seemed to lead to His greater good. Life can be a fun marathon when you run without a sack of ashes dragging along behind you. There is a wind at your back, friends cheering from the sidelines, and the freedom to take any path that comes over the horizon. I have lived that life. And I remember that books like this one didn't seem to apply to me . . . back then.

Now, I don't want to be the bearer of bad news. I can't stand negative people. Please don't call me a doom-sayer. But if for some reason, you have come this far without the ashes that come from brokenness, get down on your hands and knees and thank God. And then humbly lift your head, stand up slowly, and know that one day life will push in hard. The rings of fire will be lit, and they will begin to inch their way toward you and everything you thought made you strong.

By adulthood, I had somehow come to think that I was just going to coast on into heaven. I knew that I might lose someone I loved to death or sickness, but personally assumed that I was over the hump, so to speak. I believed that I would be able to handle trials and heartache with great maturity and wisdom . . . that everything would be spiritually easy from here on in. What I now know is just how stupid a person can still be as an adult. I will absolutely not be coasting into heaven. I will be tripping in. Out of breath and tattered from the journey. Just thankful to be there, falling on my face, skinned knees and all, right into the presence of God.

In case you have missed it, there is a battle going on. The battle is for your soul. And if your soul belongs to God, Satan will go after your heart and your mind and your passion. You will still make heaven, but eventually he will turn up the fire and try to scorch your dreams, your enthusiasm, and your very life. He will torch the foundation you've built and laugh as your hope goes up in smoke. He will add ashes to your ashes and guilt you into carrying that sack around every day of your life. As long as you and I are hauling that stuff around, Satan wins. And I'm so tired of him winning.

Ashes paralyze. Ashes make you numb. The load is tiring.

The burden is beyond description some days. We begin to shut down emotionally, mentally, and especially spiritually. Years and years pass and then one morning we just can't feel anything anymore. Empty and completely without joy or desire or ambition.

I don't know where your ashes have come from . . . abuse, addiction, failure, or regret. But what I do know is that you and I don't have to lug them around forever. Maybe you have gone numb. Maybe you are racked with pain. Maybe you have just quit trying. Maybe you are hiding underneath the pile wondering if anyone will ever come and find you.

Let me remind you . . . the One who calls you beautiful is coming to the rescue.

Binding the Brokenhearted

Sometimes it feels like everyone can see all of my sin. Sometimes it feels like the person I'm talking to has labeled me an outcast. Sometimes I beat myself up with guilt and let myself think that the flogging is deserved. Sometimes it feels like I'm doomed to hang my head for the rest of my life. No more laughter. No more peace. I am a broken person. I have emotional scars that others have given to me, and I bear the bruises of my own clumsy stumbling. Besides, there are so many ashes . . . wanna see them? I can prove it. I've got lots of them.

Do you know what the prophet Micah said about God? "You . . . *delight* to show mercy." Micah 7:18 (emphasis mine)

But our God—the God of forgiveness, the God of healing, the God of glory—is not impressed or dissuaded. He is not appalled.

He has not turned away in disgust. His heart aches to hold the brokenhearted. He longs to take you and me into His arms and cover us with His grace and protection.

Did you know that God takes great pleasure in handing out mercy? He delights in holding back what we could have deserved and what others believe we should get.

When I think about mercy I have this picture in my head: I am in an old cabin, kind of like a little house in the big woods. On this dark, winter day I am inside the cabin alone when a blizzard begins to blow against the walls that protect me. The wind and snow are whipping around the house and blowing through the cracks between the logs. The door is blown open. The snow is blinding and the wind is stronger than me. I am trying to close the door, but I can't. Just as I am about to give out, a man steps from the night into the cabin and pushes the door closed. Then he stands there until daylight, his great strength holding back the blizzard and the elements that threatened my very life. He is mercy, and he has saved me from the storm that would have destroyed me. He has held back what could have taken my life.

When God, in His mercy, comes to bind up our broken hearts, He does more than bandage the wounds. He heals them. He does more than turn on a light. He shows you things you never dreamed of seeing. He does more than pat you on the head and tell you to run along and play. He asks you to dance. When God comes to rescue His beloved, there is never anything bland or routine about His coming. He comes in glory and in strength with astounding, take-your-breath-away love and devotion.

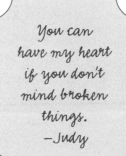

You can have my heart if you don't mind broken things.
—Judy

More Than We Deserve

I recently moved into a new house, and one day a lady came from the Welcome Wagon to leave a package of

gifts and coupons at my door. The coupons were for all kinds of things—free dry cleaning, a loaf of bread, video rentals, and more. The one I enjoyed the most was the coupon for a small flower arrangement. This little piece of paper had no value to me and would have ordinarily been regarded as trash unless I presented it to one particular florist.

For this florist, my coupon had value. I was a potential new customer and in exchange for my piece of paper, she gave me a beautiful

> Redemption:
> When God takes something worth nothing and exchanges it for something beautiful

vase of spring flowers. My coupon was redeemed. I walked into her store with a piece of paper and came out with an armful of beauty. I certainly did not deserve such a gift but was very grateful for the exchange.

That is redemption. When God takes something that seems to have no value or even seems to be a liability and exchanges it for something beautiful, we say that He has redeemed it.

Maybe your past makes you cringe at the thought of words like *romance*, *intimacy*, or *passion*. Would you let God redeem your pain and make love beautiful again?

Maybe every time I talk about dancing, you remember some old windbag yelling about the sin that can happen if you move your feet in step to music. Would you let God redeem the dance?

Maybe your life is so burdened that thoughts of dreams and aspirations seem like someone else's privilege but not yours. Would you let God redeem your disappointment and replace it with hope?

Maybe your sin is ugly and you believe that you

deserve the chains of a prisoner. Would you let the for-giveness of God redeem your choices and set you on a path of freedom?

When we fall into the presence of God with the sack of our ashes, we are not doomed to stay that way. Because of His love, God is a redeeming God. He willingly takes the burden of our ashes and replaces them with crowns of beauty. It is more than we deserve. More than we could have begged for. It is a gift, and gifts that we don't deserve are called grace.

All of Me

One day I was standing in my study, desperate for God, emptied of strength, and wallowing in my ashes. I had been pacing the floor, searching the night through the windows for something, anything to deliver me from my pain. I had played music, sung loudly, lain on my face, and prayed. I wanted to call someone, but there was no one left to call. No e-mail could give me an answer. No person could step into the room and change the circumstances. It was just me and God, and I felt incredibly alone in His presence.

Finally, I broke. Finally, I gave up. Finally, I stretched my arms up to God with tears streaming down my face and begged Him to come and do whatever it took. I think I cried something like this:

Okay, God, I give. I cannot figure this out. I cannot go on. Take all of me; please, take everything right now. Turn on Your floodlight in my soul and do not leave anything in the shadows. Lay me open and get it all out. You see the ugliness; let's deal with it. You see the flaws. You know my thoughts. You know

159

me better than I know myself, and I'm ready to show You everything.

God, I die to my dreams because I want Yours. I die to my reputation. I want Your approval. I die to my longings. You have to be enough. I just die, God. I will die to the life I have known. If the truth is going to set me free, let's get everything on the table. Whatever it's going to take, let's do it now. Break me if that's what it takes. Don't hold back. Don't string me along. Bring it on.

And God, please God, have mercy on me.

Why does it take so long to tell God the truth? Why do we wait so long to beg for mercy? Why do we hold back when freedom comes from giving up? Why do we hide the mess in our hearts when God can see it all the while? I don't know, but I do it anyway. I know better. I am a studied woman. I know about the character of God and His grace and mercy. I feel like screaming with the apostle Paul, "Why in the world do I do the things I shouldn't, when I know the right thing to do instead?"

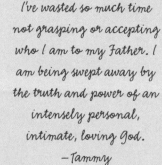

I already feel like I've wasted so much time not grasping or accepting who I am to my Father. I am being swept away by the truth and power of an intensely personal, intimate, loving God.
—Tammy

The right thing is to trust. The right thing is to tell the truth. The right thing is to walk in complete dependence on God.

The only way is to hold out what seems like such a mess . . . all of me . . . and ask for God's exchange.

The Crown

When a woman stands up at the end of a retreat and talks about the life she used to live and what God is doing for her now, she is saying, "I came to God with a worthless coupon and He redeemed it. He exchanged my sack of ashes for a crown of beauty. He replaced my despair with an unshakable hope. He keeps wiping away my tears and giving me new reasons to be glad."

Do you know any girls who wear crowns of beauty? They are not snooty. They are not pretentious. They are thankful and lovely and peaceful. Being pursued and embraced by God while you still smell like a fireplace is very humbling. These girls walk with their heads held high, yet their hearts are bowed low in reverence. They speak with the wisdom of one who has participated in the mercy of God, instead of the rambling words that come from those who have only read about Him.

They do not walk in perfection, yet they walk in confidence.

They ache for the lost and rejoice with the found. They cry with the sinners and celebrate with the forgiven. They do not walk in perfection, yet they walk in confidence. They have stood in the dark until God came to the rescue. They have jumped from the platforms of their dreams and felt His strong arms underneath them. They know God is present. They know He is able. They know more and more of the depths of His great love. They know He has asked them to dance.

Receiving a crown of beauty turns these girls into vessels of God's grace and mercy. If you have been forgiven much, you are not so quick to judge anymore. If you have been relieved of your debts, you want to release others from their bondage. If you have been lifted out of the mire of sin, you begin to look for others who need a way out. If you truly know your own weaknesses, you are not appalled by the weaknesses of others. A girl who wears the crown of beauty has begun to think and feel and give like the King of heaven. She has truly become an oak of righteousness, a radiant display of His splendor.

Do you know any girls who wear crowns of beauty? Take a minute to list the characteristics of that girl. What makes her so appealing?

_____

_____

_____

_____

Think about that girl, the one underneath the crown of beauty, the one who has been set free, the one who has traded in her ashes. Now think about yourself. What characteristics do you desire in order to be more like her? What would you do as that new girl? Have fun with this one. Dream the woman that God is dreaming in you!

_____

_____

_____

_____

_____

_____

_____

_____

_____

Probably the most powerful thing about the girl underneath the crown is that she never forgets where it came from or how it came to her. The crown was undeserved. It replaced the ashes of brokenness and pain. And in the presence of God, this girl lays her crown at His feet, the feet of the Giver, humbly grateful for His love and mercy and redemption, thankful—so very thankful—for the beauty that has come to cover her days.

Beauty for Ashes

The same offer is extended to you and to me. Amazing, I know. But doesn't it sound just like the God we've been talking about? His character is becoming apparent. He always does more. His gifts are lavish and undeserved. He pursues the woman He loves with romance and passion.

Got some ashes you'd like to trade?

The God of heaven is just waiting to see what you'll look like underneath a crown of beauty.

If there is a question attached to a girl's soul, maybe it's "Do you think I'm beautiful?" When God answers from the depth of His great love, it makes some of us feel like the wallflower who is asked to dance. But we can become distracted from His invitation because of the other loves, whispers of unbelief, noise and clutter, and because we are sometimes the prodigal, sometimes the elder brother. To return to the music and strong embrace of God requires a desperate and pursuing heart. And when a girl chooses to remain in His arms of devotion, God gives the only hope we have: His perfect love and a beautiful crown.

God is enthralled by the beauty of a woman and calls her His beloved. He wildly pursues her heart with romance and intimacy to make her His beautiful bride.

Chapter 11

His Beautiful Bride

It's early one Sunday evening in May. Candles flicker in the windows. The scent of gardenias hangs in the air. A few hundred people are hushed and peaceful. Gentle violins soothe the souls and prepare their hearts. Expectancy makes its way through the room and fills each one of us with desire. The groom enters. Smiling. Anxious. Handsome. Lovely women slowly stroll in and come and take their place in front of this audience of anticipation. And the doors are closed.

A pause in the pageantry is meant to pique our curiosity. Our longing to see. Our desire to behold. The minutes are almost longer than emotion can wait. Bells peal from the steeple and sound out the hour. An organ begins to play and strings join in. We stand and turn as the music builds and our hearts beat faster. We want to see her.

Two men push back large wooden doors so that we can finally glimpse her radiance. Eyes begin to fill with tears, and all around you can hear the whispers of delight. Everything else fades. Nothing else matters. Because before us, standing in the archway of this sanctuary, is the most beautiful woman in the world.

Veiled in splendid couture. Striking and yet serene. It seems as if everything in her life has led up to this place and that man and these witnesses. Physically, mentally, emotionally, and spiritually . . . for these few moments everything is right with the world, and everything is well with her soul.

Her brilliance fills the room. Her elegance captures every attention. She is the one we have waited for. She is the object of our admiration.

She is the beautiful bride.

The Beauty

The bride is breathtaking. She is grace and elegance. She is exquisite. She is the most glorious woman in the room. Every eye is on her. Everyone is watching. Finally, someone has noticed. The man has come to the rescue. The future looks like an exciting adventure. Life couldn't be more perfect.

Maybe you have dreamed of being the bride. I was a bridesmaid *fourteen* times before it was my turn. When you've worn that many taffeta dresses with dyed shoes to match, you've had plenty of time to think about what it would be like.

My friend Amy dreamed of being a bride ever since we were little girls. In high school, just for fun on a Saturday, she'd waltz into a bridal shop, act like a wedding was immi-

> Dream a little. What do you think the day will be like when you are the beautiful bride?
>
> _____
>
> _____
>
> _____
>
> _____
>
> _____

nent, and then try on white beaded gowns all afternoon. She'd be waited on hand and foot and leave feeling like Cinderella. Me? I tried on bridesmaid dresses . . . afraid that putting on the real deal might jinx it somehow . . . always remembering that I was just one of the girls from the king-dom, the ones who stand around the edge of the room and groove to the music . . . one of the wallflowers who never gets asked to dance. I wasn't sure it would ever be my turn.

In all those bridesmaid years, I remember wondering, *What would it be like to walk in that dress, open those gifts, and smile like the happiest girl in the world? What would it feel like to be loved like that?*

A wedding eventually came for me, and I treasured every facet of the experience. The gown, the cake, the parties, the decisions, the incredible beauty of the moment—every detail was special and fun. In some ways, my turn as the bride was more than I could have imag-ined. A wedding is an exhilarating and exhausting day that comes and goes. But the desire to be the beautiful bride lingers in the heart of a woman forever.

I don't think it's any coincidence that throughout the Bible, God uses bridal imagery to refer to the ones He loves. He calls us His bride and says that He is our Bridegroom. When we are finally standing in His presence, there will be a celebration in heaven that He calls the Wedding Supper of the Lamb. How completely He knows my soul. How well He knows that I long to be the bride. How wonderful He is to make it so, for now and for all eternity.

I'm not sure that guys grasp the depth of this imagery in quite the same way girls do. We women get this. God has set in our hearts a longing for beauty and romance. And to be called the bride is to imagine that we have finally become everything we were meant to be.

◄ *What would it feel like to be loved like that?* ▲

167

Now think about this: What if we could begin to live this life and walk through each day as if it were really true? What if we decided that when God calls us His bride, it is unequivocally, unquestionably, and irrevocably so? Can you imagine how your life would change if you really believed this stuff? If I am the bride and God is the Bridegroom, and living can mean dancing in His arms of love and passion every single day . . . then I'm there. That's what I want. Sign me up and tell me which line to get in.

There was a time in my life when I would have run away from this desire. I would never have admitted to longing for anything, much less something that seems as fluff-brained and indulgent as the desire to be a bride. But this is not fluff-brain whimsy. Being known as the bride that God longs for is a truth for thinking women to embrace. The God of heaven has spoken for you . . . He is your only hope . . . He covers you with His perfect love . . . you wear His beautiful crown.

And God says that when you belong to Him, that means He has made you His beautiful bride.

Through the Eyes of a Bride

What is it about the bride? What takes our breath away and brings tears to our eyes? What causes us to anticipate her appearance, watch the radiance on her face, linger while she dances the night away, and stand to wave until she's completely out of sight? What is it about a woman who is a bride? Actually, it's everything.

She is beautiful. Oh my goodness, is she beautiful! This is the day she has waited for. These are the moments she has planned. The dress is fabulous. Her hair is perfect. The veil. The jewels. The makeup. The nails. The gorgeous lingerie underneath. Manicured. Pedicured. Facialed and exfoliated. This woman has been styled and sprayed, straightened and smoothed. She could not be more breathtaking. She is finally beautiful and she knows it. Maybe for the first time in her life, she walks into the room and experiences what it feels like to have every eye on her.

There is something about knowing that you are beautiful. You begin to act beautiful and think beautiful. You smile a lot and move with grace. The woman who is beautiful is alluring and captivating.

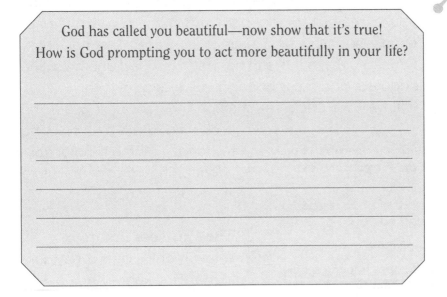

God has called you beautiful—now show that it's true! How is God prompting you to act more beautifully in your life?

_____

_____

_____

_____

_____

_____

She is confident. When a woman knows that she is a beautiful bride, you can see it in her eyes; she is confident. Brides walk down the aisle believing that they are loved and accepted and desired. And when a woman walks in that kind of truth, she is made secure. She stands a little taller. Her eyes are brighter. Her words are sure.

She doesn't have to second-guess herself. She can be decisive and strong. She leans into the moment and lets herself believe in her abilities, passions, and gifts. She is not arrogant. She is just peaceful and assured. Somebody is wild about her. Somebody calls her beautiful.

She possesses unshakable hope. Maybe more than any other time in her life, the woman who is the bride, the one who knows that she is beautiful, the woman who stands exquisitely in confidence, possesses an unshakable hope. She turns away from what has been and looks toward the future to imagine what might be.

In her confidence and beauty, the bride hears only the words of promise instead of the whispers of unbelief. She rebukes the bully of fear and trusts in the devotion she has found. The hope of a bride is steadfast. She has finally come to believe that she has been rescued and held. She is adored, and she is dancing in the arms of love.

If only we could see through the eyes of a bride. She knows that she is beautiful. She responds from the filling of confidence. She smiles at the future in unwavering hope.

The Princess Complex

A few months ago a guy said to me, "You know, Angela, you don't have a princess complex like a lot of women I know. My assistant has a princess complex, and she thinks the whole world has to revolve around her. She feigns weakness just to get attention and expects all of us to save her. She gets cold and asks everyone in the office to change the temperature.

How would you describe your hope for the future right now?

❑ No trace of hope, zeroed out, all washed up

❑ A random flicker of hope

❑ Some hope, hopeful that hope is coming

❑ God-has-my-future-and-it-makes-me-smile kind of hope!

Check out the following passages:

Psalms 62:5, 119:74, 147:11, Romans 15:4, Hebrews 6:19, 1 John 3:3.

Take some time to think about your hope for the future. . . .

She worries about her clothes and hair and jewelry. Everything has to be just right for her, but you're not like that." I smiled politely and said, "Thank you, I think."

I know that he meant that entire interchange as a compliment, but it left me aching and empty and unknown. It felt like he was saying, "You know, I don't have to worry about you. You're a big girl and you can take care of yourself. Nobody has to walk you to your car at night. No one has to lay his coat over a puddle for you. I don't have to hold the door for you or wait for you to order first. You're not like that. You are strong and self-sufficient. You go with the flow. You're practically one of the guys. Ol' buddy, ol' pal."

Gross. I am strong, but not that strong. I get things done but wish someone would come along and save me from time to time. I like guys. I like to talk to them and interact with them. But I don't want to be one of them. I want to be the girl, and I want to be treated like the girl. Secretly, I guess I really want to be a princess.

I have always thought of myself as one of the girls from the kingdom because that was the safest option. I'd never be disappointed that way. I would never have my heart broken if I lived without desire and expectation. But as I mentioned early on, the truth is that I want to be Cinderella. I want to be the wallflower on the other end of a magic wand. I want someone to be wild about me. I want to be asked to dance.

Did you see *The Princess Diaries*? The most plain and dorky girl at this particular high school finds out that she was born as a princess, sole heir to the throne. Her grandmother, the queen, has come to give her training, restyle her look, and take her back to their country to become the ruling monarch.

Initially, she balks at the whole idea. I believe her exact words were, "Shut up! Me, a princess?" She could not have more adequately expressed my sentiments in regard to princess thinking. I scream for the same reasons she did. I feel the urge to explain right in the middle of this discussion that I know I am not a princess and I don't ever expect to be treated like one. I realize we're just speaking in poetic language. It's only me, for heaven's sake. I don't walk right or talk right or look right. Hang on a minute; I'll find you some princess material, but it couldn't possibly be me.

And then, something catches in my heart. While I am busily trying to convince you that I don't have a princess complex, I feel the truth of my desire rising. I may not have the complex. I may not feel worthy or entitled, but, oh, how I'd like to be treated special. Known deeply. Loved completely. If that's a princess, yes, I'd like that very much.

Do you remember the Psalm 45 passage where God says that He is enthralled with your beauty? In the next few verses, He tells us how He treats the woman that He calls beautiful:

> All glorious is the princess within
> her chamber; her gown is interwoven with gold.
> In embroidered garments she is
> led to the king; her virgin companions follow her
> and are brought to you.
> They are led in with joy and
> gladness; they enter the palace of the king.

Psalm 45:13–15

Oh, my word, God treats the girl that He's wild about like a princess. He gives her the garments and pageantry of a bride. She lives in the palace of the King. There is no complex. This is the response of the King to the woman He calls beautiful. And she does not balk or run away. Here, the princess—who was also possibly the bride—is led into the presence of the King with joy and gladness. She receives His admiration and embraces the depth of His love for her.

So can you and I receive this imagery with the same gladness? If God calls you His bride or His princess, would you just let it be so? Can you rest in His delight for you? Would you let His longing for you cover you with peace and mercy and grace?

I know this book is a stretch for some of you . . . the whole beauty thing . . . believing that God is wild about you . . . letting your heart begin to grapple with the invitation to dance . . . desperately pursuing His heart—it's enough to make some of us feel overwhelmed. But stay with me here. Don't give up on this one.

I have friends who own socks with the word *Princess* embroidered on them, princess picture frames with crowns and scepters, and princess serving platters, but not me. The insecure one inside me has thought it would be haughty to claim princess status when I knew for sure that I was not one. But this is different. Can you hear me? Would you trust the words from Scripture? If I have to climb this mountain, I want you to go with me. God calls you and me His bride. Really. You are a princess to Him. Truly. He is wild about you. Please believe it. His love for you is unfailing. You do not have to doubt any longer.

Before you were . . . the moment God first thought of you . . . when He smiled over the purpose and plans He was making for your life—right then, He fashioned for Himself a woman that He fell in love with. A woman of

He is wild about you!

173

beauty and strength. A woman worthy of being called princess. A woman made to long for her place . . . the place of the beautiful bride.

With the fibers we have left, you and I must resolve to believe that what God has said of us is so. What are the options? To continue in doubt and disbelief until we stand before Him in heaven. And when you and I get to heaven and find out that everything God said to us was true, then what? Will we wish we had believed Him sooner? Will we regret all the years we spent in doubt and weakness?

I guess if I have a consuming fear, it would be this. I fear more than almost anything that when I get to heaven, God will say to me, "Hey, you, get in here. I've been waiting for you. But you know what? Angela, the life that I thought of when I thought of you . . . everything I had planned for you, the purpose I dreamed of, the desires and longings I wired into you—you missed most of them. You lived in fear and doubt. You wallowed around in pain and loneliness when I was calling to you all the time. I kept saying to you, 'You are My princess. You are My bride. You are beautiful and lovely to Me. You can do it. Just believe Me. I am here. Everything I have said to you is true. Jump into My arms and dance with Me,' but you missed it. So many years were wasted." If I am afraid of anything, it is the desperate fear of missing God's truth and His path for my life.

I don't want you to miss it either. I want you to know the freedom and strength that come from believing so deeply that you are left with no other option. I want you to dance in the arms of God no matter where life has you right now. In your pain. In your despair. In your loneliness. In your exhaustion. In the swirl of school and friends and family and schedules. Wherever you are, however alone you may feel, don't miss the words God wants to speak to you:

You are beautiful.
You are desired.
You are known.
You are held.
You are protected.
You are rescued.
You are forgiven.
You are pursued.
You are seen.
You are precious.
You are My princess.
You are My beautiful bride.

As you read over the words God wants to speak to you, write beside each one how God is showing you it's true in your life.

This is the heart of God for you. These are the truths of Scripture written about you and me, and therefore, my friend, they are so.

The Dance

Do you know what happens when you learn the steps to a dance? When you finally learn the steps, then you can take your eyes off yourself and look up into the eyes of your Beloved. You trip and stumble and try again until you can lift up your head and hold His gaze. When you become sure of the steps and trust in His leading, then you'll float around the room in His arms, caught up in the music and assured of His love. You can rest and enjoy.

Enjoy.

Have you been enjoying very much lately?

God didn't bring you to the dance just to have you stand around the edge of the room. There is a life He meant for you to live. There is purpose in your being here. There is passion to be enjoyed.

Remember, you have been set free for freedom's sake.

God did not bring you to the dance so that you could blend in and stand alone like a wallflower. It's time to get down with your bad self! It's time to boogie. Electric slide. Two-step.

Think about the bride at her reception. She is the beautiful woman in the middle of the room having the most fun. She is the one smiling the brightest. She is the girl every man wants to dance with. But she only has eyes for one. She wants to look into the eyes of her groom. She's polite to everyone else but wants to dance with him.

When you and I are dancing in the arms of God, we are close enough to Him to hear Him whisper. We begin to dance as He dances, move as He moves, and go where He leads. It's not so much about me anymore, it's more about us. God with me. Never alone. Intimate.

I just hung out with some really cool women in Colorado this weekend. We talked about dancing with God. We talked about what it would look like and feel like to live in His arms. I'm telling you, this stuff is contagious. When you get around someone who is dancing, you want to dance too. If you believe that you will be stuck in wallflower status all your life, I am praying that by now you know that this is the lie Satan wants you to believe. He likes for you to feel less than. He wants you to believe you're not good enough. He wants you to be hesitant and afraid. He wants you to keep saying, "I could never dance like that." He knows that your whole life will change if you choose to remain in the arms of God.

When you and I are held by God, we can trust with an unwavering trust. Last night, I took three flights all across the country to get back home. It was probably one of the worst nights of flying in my life. The pilots couldn't seem to get above or around the storms that rocked our planes.

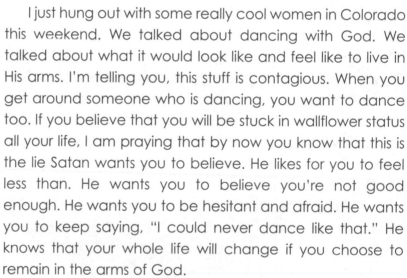

We hit air pockets and turbulence from one coast to the other. Drinks spilled. Children screamed. Everyone stayed quietly locked inside their seat belts. Friends held hands. I was by myself, and the only thing I knew to do was hang on to God. I had left no other options in my life.

I closed my eyes and prayed, *Okay, God. I know You have me. I know that I am tied on. I believe that nothing will come to me apart from Your watchful eye. I will not be afraid. You hold every single day in the palm of Your hand. I will not be in heaven until You call for me. God, just hold me close.*

After I got home around midnight and finally lay in my bed, I could still feel the tension in my hands from gripping the armrests. And yet, there was an amazing peace in my soul. God had held me all night and carried me home to safety and rest. I was so grateful and whispered thanks as I fell off to sleep.

Is our everyday life any different? Some days we are sailing through blue skies with an upgrade to first class and tailwinds behind us that gently carry us to the destination, smoothly and on time. Other days the night is dark and the rain is bitter. Thunder and lightning surround us. We sit on the runway wondering if taking off into a night like this is such a great idea. And sure enough, just as we thought, it's not much better in the air. The plane sways and lunges like the bottom has fallen out of the sky. Your hands clutch the armrest. Your body is tense. It's more than a bumpy ride. It's awful and scary.

Blue skies or dark of night, one truth still holds: God has you. And this is the promise He has made to you: He will never let you go. Will you rest your head on His shoulder and trust? Will you let Him be God so that you can be cared for? Will you stop turning away and just dance in His arms?

It's time to begin living like we belong to God.

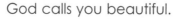

The Woman in His Arms

God calls you beautiful.

I believe you have heard Him by now.

God sees you across the room and invites you to dance.

I think that you have always wanted to dance.

God whispers His great and passionate love for you.

I believe that you long for His wild and faithful pursuit.

God promises, "I will forgive you."

You need to hear that.

God says, "I can clear out the clutter and turn down the noise."

I believe you need His help.

God shows you that He is the only hope you have.

Aren't you relieved that it's not all up to you?

God takes care of the bully of fear.

How does it feel to be rescued by Perfect Love?

God gives you a beautiful crown.

Just wear it.

God calls you His beautiful bride.

Now shine.

Maybe the time has finally come for you and for me. It's time to begin living like we belong to God. It's time to be the girl who walks into the room, beautiful, confident, and full of the hope of glory. Let Him make you captivating.

I don't know about you, but I know for myself that I've wasted enough time. Enough of the weak-willed woman. I'm done with the choices from the distant country. Too much standing around, already. I have been paralyzed by deceit long enough.

Maybe I have another fifty years left. Maybe I have five days. Either way I am choosing that each moment will be spent in the arms of God.

That's the love I was made for. That's the place I'm supposed to be. Life will never quite add up anywhere else. I'll always come up short any other way.

You can hear the music and you can feel those feet wanting to dance. So come on. You were made for this. All along, God has called you beautiful. From the very first, He has been taken with you.

Enough watching, already.

That's it.

One foot in front of the other.

One step at a time.

Find the rhythm.

There you go.

Now this isn't so bad, is it?

I knew you had it in you.

Wait a minute, I think you're smiling.

Nope, it's more than a smile.

It's something deeper.

Something more brilliant.

Can you see it?

Can you feel it?

You are breathtaking.

Yes, you.

Beautiful.

I think by now you have heard that God calls you beautiful. I believe you hear His voice calling you into His arms. I think you can just about hear the music, and you are finally willing to admit that those feet of yours can dance. So what will you do? Continue to stand around the edge of your life? Or will you get yourself on the dance floor and dance the dance of your life in His arms? Spend some time in prayer on this one. Journal. Pray. Call someone. But don't miss responding to God on this. He is inviting you to dance. What will you say?

Notes

Chapter 3

1. Taken from Brian Irwin, *Connected Hearts* (Longwood, FL: Xulon Press, 2002), 292-93.

Chapter 6

1. My gratitude to Karen Ellison and a talk she gave on hindrances to intimacy at our women's retreat, Spring 2002.
2. Ibid.

Chapter 7

1. My thanks to my pastor, Brad Brinson, for his beautiful illustration of the grain truck in a powerful sermon he delivered on this passage, Spring 2002.
2. Scotty Smith, Objects of His Affection: Coming Alive to the Compelling Love of God (West Monroe, LA: HowardPublishing, 2001), 34.

Taylor's Bio for Mom

Hey, I'm Taylor. I'm 14 years old and right in the middle of my crazy, drama-filled, teenage years. And who gets to put up with all the drama? None other than my awesome mom, Angela Thomas. Her publisher asked me to tell you a little bit about her, so here goes:

Well, I'll start off by telling you how great she looks in the morning when she wakes up. As hard as I try, she still won't show me how she gets her hair to stick up like that. "A family secret," she says. She really is a beautiful, easy-going person. Except for the occasional meltdown, she always has a smile on her face and is in a good mood. She is very funny, and all my friends love her.

My mom is a writer, and she gets e-mails and letters from people all over the world who have read her books and want to thank her. I am very proud of my mom for what she does. One of my favorite things is watching her work. I get to go with her a lot to hear her speak. It's fun to be in that atmosphere and watch her do her thing. I love it when the audience cheers her on and laughs at her jokes and gives her standing ovations. It makes me feel good for her and proud to be her daughter.

She works very hard at what she does, and when she comes home, she has to work hard all over again to take care of our family. I have two brothers (Grayson, 10 and William, 8) and one sister (AnnaGrace, 6). Sometimes they are hard to keep up with and maybe just a little annoying, but all in all, we get along pretty well.

You know how we girls always think it's the end of the world when our mom won't let us do something? I have felt like that. My mom says, "It's for your own protection." Sometimes I feel like Mom is being over-protective, but I know that it will help me in the long run. I believe that she really is just trying to take care of me. I understand that she loves me and wants me to do what's right. I respect her for that.

I love my mother to death. Not only is she my mom, but she's my best friend! I know you're going to love her too.

Taylor

For information on having
Angela speak to your group,
please contact:

Creative Trust
(615) 297-5010
info@creativetrust.com

Visit Angela on the Web at
www.AngelaThomas.com/JustForGirls

HEY GIRLS,

Angela now has a Web site just for you!!

www.AngelaThomas.com/JustForGirls

✻ **Talk** with others in community forums about seeing themselves through God's eyes.

✻ **Get** helpful insight from Angela's journal.

✻ Plus, find out about Angela's appearances, books, newsletters, downloadable **FREE** stuff and more!

YOU'RE NOT ALONE.

Learn how to live a love that is no fairy tale and to dance for eternity with a GOD who thinks, who knows, who created you BEAUTIFUL.